"To

Ralph Boyce

AGAINST
THE TIDE

Black Experience in the ILEA

Compliments

Edited by Sarah Olowe

An ILEA Commemorative Publication

AGAINST
THE TIDE

First published in 1990 by
The Inner London Education Authority
The County Hall
London SE1 7PB

Design, typesetting and production by
Hansib Publishing Limited
Tower House
139/149 Fonthill Road
London N4 3HF England. 01-281 1191

Printed by
Hansib Publishing Limited
Unit 8
Caxton Hill Industrial Estate
Hertford
Hertfordshire
SG13 7NE

Cover design – Tim England

British Library Cataloguing in Publication Data
Against the tide : black experience in the ILEA
1. Racism. Policies of Inner London Education
Authority 305.8009421

ISBN 0-7085-0022-6

Contents

PART II: In the Community

Acknowledgements

This project would not have been realised without the support of a number of individuals in and outside the ILEA. Some did more than most, but to all those who supported the project, sincere thanks.

Special thanks to members of the Steering Group: Winston Best, Trevor Carter, Yvonne Conolly, Mike Hussey, Rehana Minhas, Pauline Walsh, Sarah Olowe, Najama Shah and Anstey Rice.

Thanks also to:

Arif, for his guidance and technical assistance throughout;

Sarah, the editor, for putting up with us and the frustration;

Birthe King, for her support and initial work on the project;

Eugene Bryan, Jennifer Peck, Andrew Robinson and Sumi Tikaram for their invaluable assistance;

Kingsley Abrams, for his co-ordination and chasing;

The contributors, for their discipline and finding the time to make this a reality;

The Afro-Caribbean Research Project for their permission to reprint sections of *Black Voices – An Anthology of ACER's Young Black Writers Competition.*

Hansib Publishing, Leigh Wilson and the rest of the staff, for their assistance in making the final product something to be proud of.

The views expressed in this collection are the writers' and interviewees' own and do not necessarily represent the policies of the ILEA.

Foreword

The idea for this publication came about in February 1989 following a request by some black employees of the ILEA in response to the Education Reform Bill, enacted the previous July, with its clause to abolish the Authority. The request was for an accurate record of the development of anti-racist education in the Authority and in particular of the experiences and perspectives of black staff. The proposals were approved by the ILEA as part of its commemoration and a Steering Group was constituted. The first meeting of the group took place in April and I became the convenor.

The discussions of the Steering Group were often both interesting and stimulating. I was amazed by the group's mass of knowledge and wealth of experience. One of the tasks we undertook was to compile a long list of people, to whom invitations were then sent informing them of the project and inviting them to contribute.

The compilation was to be an exposition of the black experience with appropriate analysis. There were times when it seemed that the objective would not be achieved. However, the Steering Group remained committed and dedicated to the project and decided to press on. Neil Fletcher, Mike Hussey, Rehana Minhas and Herman Ouseley deserve a special mention for their encouragement and support. Special mention must also go to Lorna Boreland-Kelly and Les Francis who allowed me to off-load when things looked desperate and gave generous support throughout the months of co-ordinating this project.

It is not often that people attempt to tell it as it is. This anthology is an attempt to put on record the contributors' experience of working in the large and lumbering organisation which is the ILEA. The chapters in this commemorative publication are a true and accurate documentation of people's experience of struggling to influence and bring about change in a system which they found to be unjust. Those who found the time to contribute have described the difficulty of access afforded both to black and ethnic minority people working in the ILEA and to the consumers of the education service.

In part, this book is a tribute to those pioneers who, against all the odds, forced the educational establishment to address the ill-effects of miseducating black and ethnic minority children. One can but marvel at their staying power and their ability to press on when all seemed against them. It is true that few, if any, are rewarded. However, time and history will, no doubt, account for their passing. Far too often it is said that, as a people, we have no history. This work and its authors do not subscribe to that view. They believe that the long tradition of our oral and written history should continue and education should be no exception.

I cannot claim that this is a definitive work of black people's experience in the ILEA or a scientific analysis of it. It can best be described as a taster which should be savoured. This collection covers a wide range of experiences within the Inner London Education Authority, from shop assistant to politician, each with their own perception and experience. It may be described by some as a reflection of the ILEA, the Authority who, it is claimed, led the way in the promotion of anti-racism and equality of education.

As we enter this decade with the prospect of thirteen new local education authorities assuming responsibility for education in inner London, it is to be hoped that this book will serve as an invaluable reference point for the administrators on how not to do it, and as a source of inspiration to the many black brothers and sisters still engaged in the struggle *Against the Tide*.

I hope that by sharing their experiences with you the authors will inspire you to tell your story. Open the pages of this book, partake and be enriched.

Anstey A Rice
Convenor
Steering Group 'Black Experience'
Deputy Leader
ILEA

Introduction

Black and ethnic minority children account for almost half of the pupils attending inner London schools and colleges and each year, until abolition, the Inner London Education Authority spent over £1 billion teaching them. It employed over 80,000 staff to do the job but, in contrast with its users, the ILEA's policy makers, officers and teachers were mostly white. The ILEA ran London's schools for 120 years, but it wasn't until 1981 that Geen Bernard became its first black politician. This was followed by the appointment of Sylvia Denman who, as Head of the Equal Opportunities Unit, became the ILEA's first black senior officer. In 1986 a further eight black politicians were elected and Herman Ouseley, in the newly created post of Director of Equal Opportunities and Policy Co-Ordination, brought to two the number of black senior officers ever appointed by the Authority.

The picture in schools was similarly depressing save for the fact that, by the fifties, there were low-grade black teachers already working in British schools. The ILEA administered 850 primary schools; in 1970 Yvonne Conolly became the Authority's first black headteacher, but fewer than ten black educationalists went on to join her. At the time of abolition, most of the ILEA's one thousand black teachers were still in low-grade posts with little hope of promotion. Many of them were born in the United Kingdom, but selection panels continued to express surprise when they managed to speak English "without an accent".

This book is a collection of papers by those black people who worked and studied within the ILEA. Many potential contributors thought long and hard about the risk to their careers and personal welfare and decided not to participate. Those volunteers who did participate, struck perhaps by the gap between the Authority's public commitment to equality and what was actually delivered, have dwelt on mistakes and absences. Part I throws open the doors of the policy-making and administration centre at the County Hall and includes the views of the Authority's politicians, officers, inspectors and servicing staff. Part II moves from the County Hall into ILEA schools and colleges. In this section parents, teachers, governors, college administrators and students tell their version of events. In Part III, Schools Inspector Yvonne Conolly and Social Work Manager Clem Derrick give personal summaries and look to the future.

A characteristic failing of English education is that, despite its good intentions, it regards the presence of black pupils as a problem. Until the mid-seventies the buzz word was "assimilation" and the government's concern was for English to be taught to Britain's "immigrants". The ILEA responded by building off-site language centres for pupils who were understood to have language difficulties. The language centres were co-ordinated under the umbrella of the Unified Language Service and the majority of teachers employed by it were white.

In 1963 the Centre for Urban Educational Studies (CUES) was set up. Its aim was to help teachers to respond to the educational needs of pupils in urban schools by developing teaching methods and materials. Roy Truman, then a District Inspector, played a key role in establishing the Centre and was subsequently appointed as the Centre's first director. Special projects, such as the "Reading Through Understanding" project, designed to help both teachers and pupils to develop a positive attitude towards Caribbean dialects, and the "Education Liaison Pilot Scheme" which aimed to promote cultural integration by developing links between the home and the school, were set up to promote integration.

The 1976 Race Relations Act provided the mainstream support required to make further changes and, on the 8th November 1977, the ILEA Education Committee endorsed proposals which included the setting up of a new inspectorate to co-ordinate the Authority's initiatives on multi-ethnic education. The Multi-Ethnic Inspectorate (MEI), under the leadership of a white man called Bev Woodroffe, came into operation in September 1978. It inherited the management responsibilities for the teams, projects and initiatives already in existence as well as instigating its own. Some very worthwhile projects were supported. Notable examples were the Afro-Caribbean Education Resource Project, an independent venture which the Authority helped by providing staff, and the Resource Centre for Asian Studies. Both organisations compiled and produced new learning materials. The MEI also tried to influence the practice of their colleagues by publishing the *Multi-Ethnic Education Review*, a journal which addressed current debates and disseminated ideas about multi-cultural practice.

However, while this was going on, plans were under way to develop the Authority's strategy for "containment and control" of black pupils. By the late seventies over fifty schools had "sanctuaries" for disruptive children and in 1980 the ILEA launched a £1.6 million programme to provide another fifty off-site centres. This was carried out in spite of the well-publicised research of Bernard Coard and the Redbridge parents which provided statistical evidence that black children of West Indian origin were wrongly assessed and disproportionately placed in schools for the educationally subnormal.

The ILEA's delivery of multi-cultural education from 1977 to 1982 suffered from an over-reliance on the Multi-Ethnic Inspectorate and their teams, and on specific projects which did not have a clear relationship to overall curriculum development. It wasn't long before the MEI was being dubbed the "fire brigade" because of the ILEA's unrealistic assumption that it should rush in and sort out the many problems created by both the Authority's institutionalised racism and the direct racism of its personnel. For many years the MEI was a team of just five people. Nevertheless, they were expected to work across the whole curriculum, throughout all the schooling phases, as well as communicate with Community Relations Councils and the ethnic minority organisations of inner London. As well as being based on the lower rungs of the inspectorate hierarchy, its work was confined to the Schools Branch. The ILEA had seven administrative branches but the Multi-Ethnic Inspectorate's poor location meant that it could not communicate with them except via the offices of the Chief Inspector. The MEI's lack of formal authority and its inability to influence key decisions was the main reason why the MEI was not effective.

Meanwhile, the mainstream debate about black people had shifted from notions of assimilation and the value of cultural diversity to concerns about public order. The educational establishment had already addressed the problem of controlling "disruptive" black children, but it had not looked at what to do with them once they left school. Unemployment was increasing and black youths discovered that it was not only the school system that was biased against them. In 1981 there were uprisings in many of Britain's urban areas. Opinion was divided as to how best to deal with the disturbances; some politicians, on both left and right, favoured saturation policing. Others argued that insensitive policing had in most cases made matters worse – but the number of police was neither the main cause nor a solution.

In the same year as the uprising Ken Livingstone and the Labour left won control of the Greater London Council and, in response to years of grass-roots pressure, set an agenda of radical equal opportunities policies. The ILEA, then part of the GLC, began a complimentary programme led by Frances Morrell. One of the cornerstones of the Morrell programme was the formulation of an anti-racist policy and the then Director of the Race Relations Policy and Research Unit at London University's Institute of Education, Dr Chris Mullard, was asked to write the policy documents.

Chris Mullard had developed a controversial critique of post-war British education and the decision to invite a black radical academic to write the policy document was politically very significant. His understanding of racism, which he translated into the formula Racism = Prejudice and Power, provided a much-needed theoretical framework for dealing with institutional and personal manifestations of racism. Mullard's analysis did not subsume race to class, but provided a framework for race, class and gender inequalities to be addressed simultaneously. As a black educationalist he was aware of the need for involving black people in the decision-making process.

Chris Mullard's thesis contrasted sharply with the hitherto prevailing idea of multi-cultural education which encouraged the teaching of different cultures in the hope that tolerance of "minority" cultures would eventually follow. Sivanandan, in the winter 1983 edition of *Race and Class,* aptly describes the limitations of this approach.

> There is nothing wrong with multi-racial or multi-cultural education as such: it is good to learn about other races, about other people's cultures. It may even help to modify individual attitudes..but it is merely to tinker with educational methods and techniques and leave unaltered the whole racist structure of the educational system. "Ethnic minorities" do not suffer "disabilities" because of "ethnic differences" but because such differences are given a differential weightage in a racist hierarchy.

However, the evidence suggests that Mullard's views were not sufficiently supported or even comprehended by the majority of ILEA Members, officers and inspectors who usually participated in policy making and implementation. In the subsequent contest over competing definitions of socio-educational reality the cultural pluralist model refused to go away. Schools who had already formulated whole-school anti-racist policies welcomed the Authority's new policies, while black teachers' groups and trade unionists, though cynical about the Authority's commitment to delivering the policy, nevertheless saw its potential and welcomed it. However, no sooner had the anti-racist policy been endorsed by the ILEA Education Committee than it was attacked by the popular newspapers and some headteachers who saw the formulation of whole-school anti-racist policies as having no bearing on the delivery of education and opposed the policy on the grounds that it created an unneccessary workload.

This opposition was further fuelled by the writings of Tom Hastie who unwittingly epitomised the reaction of many white educationalists and politicians. Hastie, the Warden of the ILEA's Social Sciences Teachers' Centre, was a long-standing member of the Labour Party, but this did not stop him joining forces with the right on education matters. In a chapter of the radical right-wing *Anti-racism: an assault on education and value,* edited by Frank Palmer (1986), Hastie is critical of the attempts made to change the Eurocentric perspective of British history and, describing his political views, states:

> I am well aware that a number of my fellow contributors to this book do not share my political views and loyalties..in spite of these differences we share a coincidence of views on matters of intellectual honesty, and balanced education...There are some things which cut across party political boundaries.

Hastie's attacks on the ILEA's anti-racist initiatives were the beginning of concerted opposition which publicly redefined anti-racist education as political indoctrination and an attack on British "heritage" and "culture".

Some headteachers and teachers, while not explicitly adopting the Hastie position, argued that the Authority's initiatives were too doctrinaire. This position gathered popular support and was justified by the argument that teaching was a profession and teachers should therefore be trusted to treat each child as an individual irrespective of colour. Another classic response was that there was "no problem here," and that the formulation of the policy was itself divisive. There were other variations, but most arguments tended to ignore the bulk of black pupils' day-to-day experience in schools.

Battles were fought throughout the ILEA wherever genuine attempts to apply the new policy were made. In sympathetic schools, headteachers and staff met with stiff opposition from white parents (both middle class and working class), and in one or two schools white parents' groups were set up with the support and encouragement of local fascist organisations who argued that, if black parents had the "right" to meet as a group, so too had they. Meanwhile, white women teachers complained about being excluded from black teachers' meetings, apparently blind to the fact that, at the meetings they convened on gender issues, curriculum development or anything else, black people were conspicuous by their absence.

Applying a comprehensive set of new policies will predictably meet with opposition where it challenges the established power structure. In the ILEA's case, while the political will existed to vote in policies which were ahead of public opinion, insufficient thought was given to questions of implementation. The Equal Opportunities Unit was set up to help with this task, but its structural position as a non-departmental branch meant that, though it had more formal authority than the MEI, it had few routes by which to exercise it. It therefore suffered from the same fate.

The Equal Opportunities Unit was headed by a black woman called Sylvia Denman. She was placed higher up the ILEA hierarchy than the Head of the Multi-Ethnic Inspectorate but, nevertheless, the unit's struggles with the maze of ILEA bureaucracy became legendary. The Equal Opportunities Unit had no structural relationship with the Multi-Ethnic Inspectorate nor with the Inspector for Equal Opportunities Gender and so could not issue directives to any other ILEA inspectors. It was set up to act as a think-tank for Members and officers but, with the administration clearly reluctant to tread the path its politicians had chosen, its advice went largely unheeded. In fact, throughout its first year, the Equal Opportunities Unit had problems getting even basic things like offices, desks and telephones. Quite simply, it was not wanted.

After the abolition of the GLC in March 1986, a new ILEA was elected. The number of elected black Members was increased to nine and it was in this period that a new post, Director of Education (Equal Opportunities and Policy Co-Ordination), was created and Herman Ouseley appointed. Working with him, the Equal Opportunities Unit could have been significantly more effective since they were now represented at senior meetings. At the MEI Bev Woodroffe was replaced by a black man called Mike Hussey. However, neither of these measures were able to halt the administration's blocking tactics and in some ways they increased.

Restructuring plans, drawn up by the MEI to increase their effectiveness, did not get beyond the offices of the Chief Inspector, despite numerous instructions made by him for amendments. However, a section of the ILEA hierarchy did moot the creative suggestion that the MEI, if it was having problems, simply be disbanded. The Race Equality Forum, convened by Herman Ouseley, which provided a means for ILEA employees to talk to Members, was opposed. Where staff were "caught" bypassing official channels of protocol in order to effectively co-ordinate their work, the Staff Code was used by management to penalise them.

The most popular reason cited for the qualified failure of the ILEA equality initiatives is the teachers' industrial action. However, teachers in London had been involved in no-cover action over pay and conditions of service since 1974, well before the start of the initiatives. By 1984 most schools either had a one-day or no-day cover policy. In 1985, when the NUT Executive increased the pressure by instructing members not to do any work outside official working hours, the ILEA administration retaliated by selectively banning daytime in-service training. Despite co-operation from many teachers, the equality initiative was one of the main areas to suffer.

Schools were nevertheless obliged to produce individual policy statements on equality but, given that the agents for change, inspectors, governors, headteachers and teachers, were the same personnel responsible for education prior to the eighties initiatives, the quality of their policies varied. A timetable of expected change had been provided by the Authority, but there was hardly any consideration of what would happen if schools failed to keep to the timetable. The role of the divisional offices was not outlined or considered, even though most classroom teachers were affected by the actions of divisional officers and inspectors rather more than by the faceless personnel of County Hall.

The route to fair and effective education will never be primarily through an equal opportunities policy, but by generating debate in a society where racism is endemic such policies bring useful results. In the ILEA's case, a lot of energy was spent getting only a little further down the road to equality of opportunity and good education, but those pockets of people who fought hard to challenge the unjust way in which our children are taught deserve our appreciation at the very least. The ILEA was not a trailblazer but it contained many innovative and talented educationalists. Their battle will continue to be fought in every organisation where changes for equality are not in everyone's personal interest.

Sarah Olowe
Rehana Minhas, Director of the Centre for Urban Educational Studies

Part I:
In the Belly
of the
County Hall

The Policy Makers

Chair of the Authority

Les Francis

Les Francis is a Labour Party Member for the constituency of Eltham. He has five children and has lived in Greenwich with his wife, Edna, for over twenty years. Mr Francis works as a driver attendant for Greenwich Social Services.

I n 1983, after years of lobbying and countless hours of hard work, something actually happened in the ILEA. The very first major constructive action relating to inner London's black population, the Ethnic Minorities Section, was formed. It comprised twenty Members: ten Afro-Caribbeans and ten from the Asian community. These twenty people elected by community groups were then accepted as a section of the Equal Opportunities Sub-Committee, from where they were co-opted on to various other sub-committees.

It is from this time on that one can really say that all aspects of equal opportunities began to be taken seriously; but not without covert and, in many cases, overt opposition. Some officers disregarded the contribution of black Members or refused to accept that racism and/or sexism were evident in their departments.

In the 1986 local elections, when the ILEA became a free-standing education authority, nine black Members were elected, three black women and six black men; all were Members of the Labour Party, which had a majority of forty-six. Five of the black Members, three women and two men, had had experience in the previous administration. All black Members were elected by the Labour Group to positions of responsibility; from deputy leaders and vice-chairs of committees to chairs of sections and panels.

Like most majority Members, my work centred on the need for high achievement for all pupils or scholars. I believe this can only come about through the medium of equal opportunities. As Vice-Chair of the Equal Opportunities Sub-Committee from 1986, with special responsibility for race issues, I concentrated on the development of policies, committing the various departments to look at their recruitment, training and operating practices in order to avoid unfairness to black and ethnic minorities. These were recorded and published as equal opportunity statements and required the creation of monitoring mechanisms and evaluating procedures.

Because of entrenched negative attitudes and working practices, many bitter battles were fought with the minority party Members. The implementation of decisions was frustrated by both the approach of management circles and obstruction by some Members of staff, as well as by the endless rounds of consultation and negotiation with the very large and varied workforce under multiple trade union representation.

I have participated in the selection of many senior staff and have both sat on and chaired grievances and appeals panels. In 1987-88 I was elected to the position of Vice-Chair of Headteacher Appointments. I wanted to appoint more black and ethnic minority headteachers, but I found that the obstacles were mostly in the earlier stages of the selection process. In 1987-88 I chaired the Joint Committee for Members and Schoolkeepers (JCMS). This position alternates annually between Members and staff-side representatives. I took this job with a view to influencing the recruitment of black and ethnic minorities and women into the schoolkeeping service. This category of work was the most complicated of the ILEA's service in which to initiate change and, I believe, the most challenging. Being a kind of negotiating forum, there was more scope for resolving issues promptly and therefore immediate satisfaction could be experienced.

In 1988-89 I was elected the Authority's Vice-Chair and in 1989-90, as the last Chair of the ILEA, I made history by becoming the only black Chairperson the Authority has ever elected. With abolition imminent, the ethos has changed as more and more priorities have been reassessed. Emphasis and momentum have been lost and energies dissipated with the need for Members to be involved with local borough education plans. As officers have dwindled, support for the Members has decreased, and information has become more difficult to obtain. This has caused frustration and delays in resolving issues.

On the whole, policies were not implemented totally because there were so many agencies and departments that had to address the issues as they related to themselves. Contrary to myth, this has little to do with the size of the Authority. The boroughs of inner London will come to realise this as they take responsibility for education.

My experience is that there is no chance of ever satisfying all the users of a service. As far as black Members are concerned, it is difficult to explain to the black communities and black staff that some changes cannot be made immediately. There is always the conflict between wanting to do something and having to accept the dictates and narrow confines of the statutory and legal obligations within which Members are required to work. Procedures have to be adhered to, not only in legal terms but because of the chaos which would result from variation.

Black Members could have been more effective had the co-ordinating efforts of some not been thwarted by people who were unable to work collectively. We have been, in effect, passengers. This is not to say there were no white Member passengers as well.

It is my belief that progress was made on a wide range of issues tackled by those Members who had the stomach to face up to problems instead of distancing themselves and resorting to destructive criticism. Individualism, a "holier-than-thou" attitude, and the desire by some to make pretty speeches regardless of the damage done to industrial relations, political cohesiveness or academic research, also thwarted progress.

I would like to express appreciation to all members of staff and elected Members who struggled long and hard for positive change and high achievement.

Deputy Leader

Anstey Rice

Anstey Rice is a Labour Party Member for Lewisham East. He began his working life as a psychiatric nurse and is presently Race Equality Officer in the Social Services Department of the London Borough of Hammersmith and Fulham.

During the run-up to an election campaign, prospective candidates have to sell themselves to various wards and constituencies. I went to Streatham, Greenwich and Lewisham East and was contacted by Putney, Dulwich, Deptford and my local party, Peckham. It was important for me to declare my support for black sections. I also talked about wanting to see more nursery education and a co-ordinated approach to anti-racist education as a whole.

I quickly discovered that selling oneself to a canny electorate is often very difficult, but was heartened by the warm response from black residents in Lewisham East and Southwark. I am grateful to the people who helped me out during that time; Errol Reid did more than most, and deserves a special thank you.

The first opportunity the black candidates had to explore where we were politically and plan a strategy was a meeting in Lambeth Town Hall. There were marked differences in our political perspectives and experiences. I was perhaps the most ardent of the black sections "supporters" among us. Other colleagues offered low-key support while some candidates were opposed to black sections altogether. Eventually we agreed which positions we would seek and how we would support each other.

The nine successful black candidates were the ILEA's first. Four of us had little or no knowledge of how the system worked, while the others had already been co-opted Members on the then Equal Opportunities Sections. I enjoyed being a backbench Member because I wasn't obliged to follow any line. Most of the time, however, I felt impotent and the same is as true today as it was back in May 1986. In May 1987 I became Vice-Chair to the Trading Supplies Sub-Committee, and in 1988 succeeded Bernie Wiltshire as Deputy Leader.

My predecessor, had he contributed, would no doubt have detailed the many battles he had with officers; in particular with the then Chief Inspector. To be treated with contempt by officers is not a pleasant experience but, as new Members of the ILEA, this was our lot. Only the in-crowd were given access to information – the rest of us fought hard to get it.

Pointing the accusing finger became a regular pastime in the early months of the first year, and the Labour Group responded by going away for a weekend to set a political agenda and find ways of improving communications between ourselves and the officers. We partly succeeded in opening up communications but somehow lost the rest. Officers were given the new policies to implement but they rewrote them instead. The policies came back to us in "officer-speak", and we found ourselves forced into what they wanted us to achieve rather than what we wanted as politicians. Four years on, I am still awaiting responses from officers to enquiries I made in 1985.

Throughout the first year, attempts were made to establish a black caucus within the Labour Group. However, it wasn't until the 1987 leadership battle that anything resembling one was actually achieved. During this time black Members were seen as power brokers, so after a number of discussions I drew up what amounted to a charter of demands. This became our bargaining position and both contenders for the leadership pledged their support to us. Neil Fletcher won by one vote.

The change of leadership saw the officers taking a more directive role in the management of the Authority and the Members became more and more like surrogate officers. Even though I only voted for her after intense lobbying, Frances Morrell's defeat as Leader of the Authority was a disappointment to me. Though she did little to help the Labour Group establish a cohesive strategy and philosophy, the loss of her skill and political agility shifted us into low gear.

Black Members' contributions are often completely ignored by officers unless they are validated by one of our white comrades. This avoidance takes place in Labour Group meetings, Leaders' meetings and Sub-Committee meetings. What is worse is that some officers ignore our existence. In August 1989, at the height of the programme to recruit teachers from Europe, the senior officers responsible didn't think it necessary to keep me informed on the progress of the exercise. The Leader, Neil Fletcher, wasn't able to attend the welcoming reception held at County Hall and the only other Member invited was the Chair of the Schools Committee – even though I was not only available but actually in the building at the time. The inherent racism in this act is self-evident. I instead found myself being called upon to give radio interviews on the matter without a brief from the Recruitment Office. When I raised the issue with senior officers, a lame and pathetic excuse was offered.

The ILEA claims to be the leading Authority in the implementation of equal opportunities, but it has failed to make appropriate use of positive action to recruit and promote black and minority ethnic people to managerial positions. In fact, it took two years for the Authority to complete the simple task of placing a job advertisement in a paper to attract more black people to the ILEA's Psychiatric Social Work Service. The advertisement used Section 5 (d) of the Race Relations Act and appeared in October 1989.

In the face of this it isn't hard to understand how Members collude with officers in the abuse of the Authority's black officers. One example: many Members were concerned about some aspects of the Youth Service. The Service was managed for years by white officers, and little was done to investigate the matter. On the appointment of a black Director for Community Education, he was thrust into a situation which was already so intense that he was assaulted. On another occasion he was asked to investigate allegations of racism at a club over which the ILEA had no real authority. This pattern repeated itself throughout the organisation. Whenever there was a problem and a black senior member of staff available, they would be thrown in to resolve it.

An " A Team" of sorts, but an " A team" without due recognition of their professional abilities. The black Members did little in these situations but express their deep concern. Perhaps we could and should have been much more effective as a power block in the day-to-day running of the Authority, but for various reasons that never happened.

The few individuals on whose behalf I intervened successfully perceived me as having a lot of power; although I would like them to hold on to that, the bulk of my power was illusory. I saw my role as accepting my responsibility to serve the community. The sacrifice has been great. This period has virtually destroyed most of my personal relationships and has reminded me that the fight against racism becomes greater the closer you are to the eye of the storm.

The most controversial issues during the last few years of the ILEA's life was the Teacher Redeployment Programme. The exercise was designed to transfer surplus teachers to schools where there were staff shortages. Once teachers had been marked for relocation they were informed but continued to teach in their original school until another one was found for them. One of the most depressing aspects of the programme was the time it took to relocate some teachers. The process often took several years and one teacher was only relocated after the intervention of both myself and the Chair of the Staff Sub-Committee. I supported the policy wholeheartedly but not its application, which I believe worked against black teachers. The promise of the Education Officer, David Mallen, to resolve the matter was never realised.

Members were regularly forced by officers into making decisions which they then had to defend publicly. One such decision was the naming of schools at risk. I found it strange that officers had been concerned for a number of years about the performance and management of a number of schools but had singularly failed to take appropriate action; that is until the pronouncement of death was passed on the Authority. Then the same officers who were responsible for the oversight of the schools suddenly spoke out. In retrospect there was probably some collusion between the officers and a handful of Members, but most of us only became aware that the Authority had issued a public statement about the schools when journalists broke the news. I discovered that political judgement was not a strong point of ILEA Members in a crisis; too many colleagues, fired up by publicity and their own egos, contributed to the negative press coverage. Against this background I faced the sharp and incisive wrath of teachers and the many black consumers of the education service. However, once I explained my position, people were warmer and more supportive.

The struggle in the eye of the storm is a continuing one for oppressed people; a struggle which has taught most of us the art of survival. My biggest disappointment in the ILEA has been our inability to maintain our strength and unity despite our political differences. But amidst the pain, there has been some joy too. Support and encouragement from the following people made things a lot easier, and included among them is my political mentor who kept on saying 'Must try harder': Lorna, Lennox, Winston, Errol, Joel, Jenny, Navelette, Eve, Peter, Sister T, Rehana, Najma, Farah, Marc and more recently Kingsley. In spite of their support, I watched helplessly as the ILEA neutralised the effect our black brothers and sisters had on the system. Look out for signs of overload: should you notice them you will know you are but a small cog in a big wheel. Nuff said, and so to bed.

Chair of the Equal Opportunities Sub-Committee

Lorna Boreland-Kelly talking to Sarah Olowe

Lorna Boreland-Kelly is a Labour Party Member for the constituency of Norwood. She has been Chair of the ILEA's Equal Opportunities Sub-Committee since 1986 and as a co-opted Member of the Authority was the Vice-Chair of the Sub-Committee prior to being elected.

I went to school in Jamaica before coming to England. At my first school in this country I was treated like a zoo exhibit because I was the only black child. There weren't all that many black people in Croydon in those days and after a lot of very negative experiences I was transferred to a Catholic school where I coped much better.

Academically, I found that standards in the Catholic schools in England and Jamaica were similar, but expectations at the state school were much lower. The Catholic school accepted the reports from my school in Jamaica. This did not happen in the state school and I was put into the D stream. At the religious school, black people were seen as part of the wider Catholic family – which was certainly better than not being valued at all.

I first became a co-opted Member of the ILEA because I was dissatisfied with my own children's education. I've had to push for adequate nursery education, I've had to push for adequate primary education, I've had battles with my children's secondary schools. In fact, the only bit of their education that I've not had to fight through is my son's further education because his college is very helpful and very good.

I recognised from day one that being a Member for the ILEA wasn't going to be a piece of cake, but I didn't realise the magnitude of the problems. The ILEA is divided up into parliamentary constituencies and there are two Members per constituency. What stands out most from my time as a black Member is that we have had to fight the bureaucracy to achieve most of what we have wanted.

Every organisation, regardless of size, must continually review its policies and machinery. Since we were elected in 1986, Members have managed to refine the grievance procedures so that they recognise the real dilemmas in which staff find themselves. Grievances against the ILEA usually involve not being appointed or shortlisted, or being appointed and then being undermined by management or other workers. Formerly, people who felt that they'd been racially harassed or sexually discriminated against found it so difficult to prove their allegations that they tended to resign instead.

Community groups often feel that you as a black Member haven't done enough for them, especially in terms of pushing for things like grants. We've had to try to get these groups to recognise that we have to work through a system – and while black Members can try to ensure that there aren't artificial blockages in the system, community groups still have to comply with the ILEA's requests and need for accountability. Last year, when the Authority decided to change the way voluntary groups use ILEA premises, black and ethnic minority groups found themselves having to pay large sums of money for the use of our premises. Les Francis and I, with the help of other colleagues, were able to ensure that they, as well as other London-wide groups, got free letting. It seems that when things go wrong the public looks to us, the Members, rather than to the appropriate officers. As Chair of Equal Opportunities I try to make myself accessible to my own constituency and to all the community groups in our ten divisions. This means I am out working most evenings.

Eight of the forty-five Labour Members are black and there is a hard core of about five of us. We have our political differences but by and large we work very well together. I think other Labour Members tend to give us more support if they see that we are speaking with a united voice. There are also some particularly supportive and sympathetic white people. In this respect both the past and present Chairs of Finance, the Chair of Schools and the Chair of the Staff Committee stand out. Of course, it has to be recognised that many of the things that we have been able to do would have been impossible had the Labour Group as a whole been blocking them. But despite majority Labour Group support, there are still a significant number of white Labour Members who oppose for the sake of opposing – which says something about their inherent racism.

When the government makes changes in legislation the ILEA has to change its policies. This is often a very fraught time because people then see you implementing legislation and not keeping to the administration's manifesto which majority party Members were elected on. It is interesting to look at the compromises Labour Members make in order to stay legal. Personally, I've always made it quite clear that as a black person I am not prepared to break the law. When we do, it is always us who come off the worst.

My experience of the Authority's officers is that they usually listen to us if they see we are supported by other Members. However, in terms of equal opportunities, we tend to have to talk to them as if they are children. When you think of the level at which officers are working, and compare that with their ignorance, it is frightening. We've had to drag the Chief Executive into countless petty issues because it has proved impossible to solve them through the proper channels and consequently they have just got bigger and bigger. For example, a black woman was encouraged by her inspector to change jobs on the understanding that she would keep a special allowance entitlement. He did this without checking and, when the worker started losing her allowance, did nothing about it. Personnel should have been able to sort that out fairly easily, but instead it went on and on, and in the end it came to me as Chair of Equal Opportunities. We had it sorted out in a day – but to do that I had to talk to the Director of Personnel. The Director of Personnel shouldn't have had to get involved, and certainly I, as Chair of Equal Opportunities, shouldn't have had to get involved.

Part of the problem with racism is that it is often easy to see things and think, 'Oh well, this could have happened to anyone.' But the inspector involved with the earlier example made the comments about the woman keeping her allowance because he knew that it was the only way they were going to get her to change jobs. Had the same thing happened to a white worker, she would have gone straight to her trade union. Inspectors and other managers know that, with black people, that sort of action is less likely.

Each employee from senior management downwards has a responsibility to ensure that the Authority's equal opportunities policies are carried out. Since 1987 we have tried to assess whether this has been happening by making each department accountable to the Equal Opportunities Sub-Committee. Each department produces equality statements which show the make-up of their workforce. They also have to show how they meet the needs of their employees and what measures they take to recruit a more representative workforce. Statements are issued annually after which we meet with the relevant department to assess its progress.

With something as sensitive as Equal Opportunities, the "bull-in-the-china-shop" approach no longer works because people have developed effective strategies for blocking that approach. We have to be at least as clever as the people we are up against and we have to be aware of the different ways in which workers in the Authority are undermined. We are coping with the organisation's racism, but we are also coping with the organisation's sexism and people can play a variety of games. A couple of years ago I dealt with a case where a black student was in the process of being expelled from his college. When we got to the bottom of what was going on, we found that the student in question had had a relationship with a female member of staff, the relationship had ended, and when he sought to resurrect the affair she had accused him of having a sexist attitude towards her. We also have cases of alleged racism between children reported to us by their schools. A child may indeed have said something that it has picked up from somewhere and doesn't fully understand, but that isn't racism.

I have said everyone *should* take responsibility, but what you find are pockets of people pushing for equality. Demands for equality come from parents and community groups, and there are still people within the organisation who are quite good at firing and pushing, despite being worried about their future after abolition.

I am currently employed as a social worker and am able to commit so much of my time to the ILEA because I get public service leave. Having had two babies since 1986 has also been helpful because this has meant two spells of maternity leave when I have been able to come in full time. I work nearby so I'm able to come in at lunchtime. In the evenings I usually work through until 11 pm or midnight. I've worked like this without a break since 1984. Come April 1990 I am going to have a long rest.

Chair of Further and Higher Education

Paul Flather

Labour Party Member Paul Flather represents the constituency of Tooting and is a former Chair of the ILEA's Further and Higher Education Sub-Committee. He is a freelance journalist and is currently working on a PhD in Indian Politics.

I n 1986 my overriding impression as a newly elected Member was that the Authority was committed to taking up black people's cases. Of course, it did not always succeed – but the ILEA, as the last vestige of the GLC, had a genuine commitment to equal opportunities policies. However, as the bureaucracy continued to discriminate against black people it soon became clear that intentions and policies do not necessarily produce results.

Once elected, the black Members were largely left to work in separate sections of the Authority. In my first year, as Vice-Chair of the Further and Higher Education Sub-Committee (FHE), I pursued issues such as the promotion of access courses and the monitoring of ethnic minority intakes in polytechnics and colleges. Then as Chair of FHE I continued to protect the range of courses and the idea of access and concessionary fees for disadvantaged people. For a while the nine black Members did hold regular meetings – though with variable attendance. Our responsibility for the ILEA as a whole meant there was little time to do specific work on black-related issues. However, as the only Asian-origin Member, I was thrown into taking up a number of key black issues. Among them was the ILEA multi-cultural Ramayana project – a cultural programme for pupils based on the Hindu epic, involving some 10,000 ILEA pupils. It was a notable success, though much of my time was spent chasing the project through the bureaucracy and continually ensuring that the allocated funds were not clawed back.

In retrospect I believe the ILEA always set out on a positive, pluralist approach to black issues, an approach which recognised the rights and needs of different communities. This often involved major policy initiatives which have left an important legacy.

On an individual level, I was involved in a number of staff grievances which concerned allegations of racism. Some cases occurred simply because procedures had not been explained or adhered to, causing distrust and confusion – but no simple generalisation is possible. I recall being "caught" in a range of black issues: mediating in a row at South Bank Poly involving the Afro-Caribbean Society, who wanted to ban the Zionist Society; rejecting complaints from the Muslim High Commission that the ILEA Ramayana project be dropped because it promoted Hindu ideas; supporting the Chinese community in its outrage over the Tiananmen Square massacre; and urging leading British Asians to do more for the disadvantaged Asians in the East End. In the past the ILEA has had difficulty reaching out to the genuine Asian community. Unfortunately, the Authority's attempts to bridge this gap, using the system of co-opted Members, was never really more than cosmetic.

We have left a special legacy in our colleges and polytechnics: detailed systems of monitoring and detailed equal opportunities statements and appeals procedures. These procedures, which were praised in national reports and by the DES (Department of Education and Science), are now being used as models elsewhere. Of course, the ILEA *should* have made the running – but at least it did not shirk the task. Overall the success must be attributed to the Members – black Members. Officers, though often willing, were easily deflected from actually implementing policies and meeting deadlines. It was repeated and continual pressure from waves of Members that, in the end, delivered up positive results.

The First Politician

Geen Bernard talking to Sarah Olowe

Geen Bernard became the ILEA's first black Member in 1981. She now represents the constituency of Bethnal Green and Stepney and is a Labour councillor for the West Thornton Ward of the London Borough of Croydon. Councillor Bernard has six children and is a single parent.

I am a qualified social worker and I do a lot of community work. I worked for Southwark Social Services for ten years until they felt that my style of social work among black families – trying to help them get back on their feet – was not what they wanted. They preferred the traditional social work which says that black people are subnormal, inadequate and inferior to whites. As a result they brought a lot of trumped up charges against me. They claimed that as an ILEA Member I couldn't do social work, so my public duty, which I was supposed to do like any white councillor, was brought into question. I believe I was sacked because I had reached the stage where I was actually level with white people, doing the same things that they were doing. They don't want to see black people at that level, it conflicts with their racism.

Community work involves picking up local issues and helping people to help themselves. It is discussing with people, listening to people and directing people into the right channels. It is not sitting in a building. If I am in the middle of Brixton market I do community work. If I go to Bristol there will be someone who can identify me as a counsellor. I'll be seen reaching people, talking with them, meeting with them, directing them and educating them.

I came through Peckham the other day and saw a black woman picking up food off the ground and eating it. I said, 'No! Don't eat it! Here is some money, go and buy some food', but she was too far gone to understand what I was saying. No child has left Jamaica to come to Britain to eat out of the white man's dustbin. We have a lot of cleaning up to do in our community.

How do you take what is inside and bring it out and put it on the table and say: 'This is me'? The black male will try but the system will now allow it. The system says: 'You're a nigger, you stay down.' He becomes angry inside and destroys himself, because that is the only way. Out of every one hundred black men I would say that seventy-five per cent have turned their anger into double-anger. When that thing inside says 'I have dreams' and your dreams can't come true it is stifling. You can't kill it.

One of the things the establishment is trying to do now is make the black kids who were born here think they are better than black kids who came here from the Caribbean and Africa. It chooses some blacks who were born in Britain and puts them into a white world. But it doesn't work. There are some black people who think they can fit into the world, but if you look at their hairstyles, their clothes, everything, they're desperate. You don't change what you are by mixing with other people. Once these black people arrive at the top, they realise they are starved of certain essentials like consciousness and knowledge of the inner self. Deep down they know that this deprivation cannot go on indefinitely.

After being sacked from Southwark Social Services a year ago I earned a living by running a Caribbean restaurant (Francellas) in Streatham. Since I opened it in 1987, I have had a lot of problems with the police. All black businesses suffer from racism and many are only surviving because they are using white people to front their shops. That option is out for me because it is against my principles.

Most white people don't like my politics. They think: 'Geen has reached the top of the ladder, why doesn't she come in and

be white, think white and act white?' Instead there is hatred
in my heart. They have robbed me of my birthright, they have
dug me out of the womb of Africa, they have destroyed my
cultural identity. I have a lot to hate them for but I have never
done anything to them.

I was invited to be a co-opted Member on the ILEA in 1981.
When I first went there any black person you saw was either
working in the canteen or doing the cleaning. I immediately
recognised that there was a need for black people to get
involved at a higher level in the education of their children
and I called for support from the black community. For two
and a half years we campaigned, canvassed and had meetings
all over the country in an attempt to get the ILEA to accept
that it was a racist institution and needed to change. I got good
help form officers. Bryn Davies was then Leader of the
Authority, and after Bryn Davies, Frances Morrell. From 1981
to 1986 I was Vice-Chair of Schools Sub-Committee. Together
we worked to achieve a better deal.

I was lucky, and after two and a half years we established a
Black (Ethnic Minorities) Section in the ILEA of which I was
Chair. We had twenty Members, two from each of the
Authority's ten divisions. Two of us sat on each of the
Authority's committees – it worked quite well. One of the most
important things we did was to help the schools' psychological
departments understand the effect they were having on our
children. At the time black children were being classified as
EBD (Emotional Behavioural Difficulties) and ESN
(Educationally Sub-Normal). So-called EBD and ESN children
were taught on off-site units. In contrast to the schools, off-site
units had no curriculum and were housed in sub-standard
buildings with inadequate teaching staff. Most black kids
between the fourth and fifth year would end up in there, girls
and boys. These kids would not be able to sit examinations.
White institutions are white spiritually and they expect black
people to be white, spiritually, socially and in every way. They
do not see you as either an individual or as a nation with an
ideology or culture of you own. The Schools' Psychological
Service was no exception. The ILEA agreed that there was
something seriously wrong, and black people worked with
officers to bring about a better understanding between our

norms and white norms.

After the election in 1986 we had nine black Members in the ILEA. But what frustrates me is the fact that when we became nine we started to fight among ourselves. One of the first things that happened was a black elected Member agreed, behind my back, to abolish the Black (Ethnic Minorities) Section. I went in one day to find that the Black (Ethnic Minorities) Section, which took me two and a half years to set up, had been abolished. There was no discussion with me even though I was the Chair. The other black Members though they had power, which I believe was why some of them were so quick to want to destroy the Black (Ethnic Minorities) Section, but their actions were not very intelligent. They should at least have waited to see the effect nine elected Members could have had.

I still believe the Ethnic Minorities Section was a good structure, something that could have gone further. Croydon now has a Black and Ethnic Minorities Section and the unions are talking about having black sections, so it was ahead of its time. What the average person doesn't know is that by the time the policy reaches him or her for so-called consultation, the decision has already been taken. I fought so that black people could be involved in the thinking stage of the policy-making. I am disappointed with this present Labour Group, but I'm more disappointed with the black group because it didn't stick together. Before the black Members were elected it wasn't as hard to get what I wanted. Now when I go to the Labour Group and put forward a motion I find a black person stands up and opposes me. It's alright all of them coming now, when the battle is won, but where were they when there was just Les Francis, Irma Critchlow, Jim Mthethwa and myself.

The biggest regret of my life is that I came to England. I'm here twenty-seven years and with the hatred that's built up in me and the way that I detest this society for what it has done to my people, I can never feel at home in Britain. I have a lot of nice friends, but when your own people are fighting against you and what you stand for, when they know that's the only way forward for the black kids, the whole thing becomes hard to stomach. My time in the ILEA was a great experience. I would do it again. But, since Frances Morrell left, nothing has been done for black kids.

We can save some of our black kids if we can afford to set up our own schools. I'd like to see schools where black teachers are heads and which take in kids from the whole community. The drive to make a black kid a white kid through education is disturbing. But I won't give up. Our ancestors put up a good fight. My parents put up a fight and I put up a fight. My children will put up a fight and my children's children's children, because you can kill Geen, but you can't kill Geen's ideology.

Turkish Non-Elected Member

Sherife Mustafa talking to Sarah Olowe

Sherife Mustafa is the Development Advice Worker at the Turkish Education Group. Since 1987 she has been a co-opted Member of the ILEA. She went to school in Islington and Haringey.

I got in this morning to find the whole building had been ransacked. All the files had been turned out. The envelopes had been torn open, the cupboards were broken and my desk drawer had been forced open. We have been burgled on three separate occasions since we moved here in March 1987.

Our organisation was founded in February 1981 and is based in Islington. It was originally funded by the GLC. In November 1986 a small amount of money was made available from the Community Education Section of the ILEA, but currently the ILEA are our major funding body.

We've found that lots of schools are in need of mother tongue support. We also teach Turkish as a second language. There are very few resources available for teaching Turkish, so one of the things our teachers are trying to do is develop teaching aids we can both use ourselves and make available to schools. We often get requests from infant school teachers asking for flash cards to greet parents when the kids come to school. We are also one of the few suppliers of Turkish literature.

The founders of our organisation felt that the high rate of under-achievement of Turkish-speaking children in schools was not being addressed. Originally, people helped each other on a voluntary basis. If a child needed to change secondary school, an English-speaking relative would go down to the Education Office and do the relevant paperwork. Now people are starting to get used to coming to the Turkish Advisory Education Group and having that done for them.

This is a three-borough project: Hackney, Islington and Southwark. Within the ILEA, Southwark has the largest number of Turkish-speaking people. But we provide a service to people from all over the ILEA. In Greenwich, for example, the John Roan Secondary School wanted us to help them in finding a Turkish teacher for their school, so we went to meetings and found a tutor for them.

When bilingual young people show an interest in working in an educational organisation, we let them experience the kind of work that they would do if they were a normal member of staff. We also help university students with their research because there is very little educational material available on the Turkish-speaking community. As well as these activities, and as a matter of goodwill, we advise overseas students. They bring lots of money into the ILEA's institutions, so we try to give them the best advice about which courses are suitable for them.

A few years ago the ILEA's Members decided that, because of the particular needs of the Turkish and Bangladeshi communities, they would co-opt two minority Members. I was chosen by the Education Committee. At first I was overwhelmed by the reports and the system, and in retrospect it would have been nice if there had been some kind of training for co-optees. We were given very little introductory information; just thick handouts and loads of information on our legal liability.

I know that both myself and the person who originally became the Bangladeshi co-optee felt that we were always on the periphery and could never get properly involved. It's very difficult to combine a demanding job with being an active Member, especially when there are party political Members who see it as their full-time job. To be honest, I still don't know which Member is which.

I know the system well enough because I have a good rapport with officers in the Equal Opportunities Unit. But I found the level of debate in the Committee to be minimal. There is never the time to ask what is going on because the agenda is so heavy. I have tried to be fair to myself and have abstained if I did not understand the issue. Mostly, I have to stick to recommendations.

Myself and the Bangladeshi co-optee were each designated a Committee as well as both being on the Equal Opportunities Committee. This entailed quite a lot of meetings. The ILEA's Education Committee, which is held every six weeks, is where all the Members meet together. Sitting through two to three hour meetings is very alienating when you feel you are not being productive or making any significant input.

It's fair to say that a certain amount of responsibility lies with me, but my first and lasting impression was that the majority of people knew the ropes. We, as co-opted Members of the Authority, were not people who had previously been involved in the top tier of the decision-making mechanism. It doesn't matter how articulate or how interested you are, if you don't understand the system and the way that it functions you can't make a positive contribution.

Afro-Caribbean Non-Elected Member

Vince Scantlebury

Vince Scantlebury is the parent of a student currently at a college run by the ILEA and is a co-opted Member of the Authority's Education Committee.

Having been educated in the West Indies, I understand why children, especially those from the Caribbean community, are failing in the British education system despite all the efforts of the ILEA to improve the quality of education it provides. The basic philosophy of education in the West Indies is that all children leaving school at the age of sixteen should be able to read, write, spell and count satisfactorily. In my experience of British state education, emphasis is on experiential learning. This, I believe, can only be effective if the basics of English grammar and mathematics are taught properly in primary schools. At the moment, not only do a significant number of pupils leave school with GCSE grades 'D' or below, but they are unable to spell and count properly. How can this group of pupils expect to get an interview for a decent job? They often end up on a Youth Training Scheme.

Various studies on supplementary schooling suggest that students who attend supplementary schools are able to grasp the "three Rs" better than those who do not attend. In very few of my official visits to schools have I experienced activities involving mental arithmetic or spelling and I have noticed children's work with extremely poor spelling.

The majority of schools I have visited have had no overall school policies or no future planning on schemes of work. Secondary schools work to syllabuses and not to have a proper scheme, or in some cases a record of work, is inexcusable. Having taught in further education for over twelve years, I am convinced that if the Authority had paid more attention to my advice on these issues there would be some improvement in the performance of students in both primary and secondary schools.

When I was studying for my GCE 'O' levels and my postgraduate Certificate in Education, both the teaching and resources provision were generally very good. Now, however, due to recent budget cuts, resources have appreciably deteriorated. As a member of the Inspection and Learning Resources Section (ILRS), which specifically looks at HMI and the ILEA Inspection reports, I am very unhappy about the way these cuts have affected the overall effectiveness of some schools. Problems such as poor toilet facilities and updating library books and computers are only the tip of the iceberg that schools will face after the abolition of the ILEA in 1990.

The ILEA's policies on equal opportunities are the best in the country. In my opinion the Authority is a leader in social provision and the work of officers and Members is commendable. Black Members, in particular, have progressed to influential positions: chairs of sub-committees and Chair and Deputy Leader of the Authority. No other education authority has been able to emulate this, despite claims of non-racism. The support the ILEA has given to black organisations is typical of their belief in equal opportunities and is possibly the envy of other education authorities. However, I feel that the Authority could have done more to ensure that the proportion of black headteachers reflected the balance of their schools.

I would like to thank all those parents, officers and Members of the ILEA for giving me the chance to play an active part in one of the best education authorities in the country. When education is handed over to the boroughs in April 1990, I believe that a significant number of people, including black Members of the Authority, will remember it with pride for years to come.

Officers

Head of the Equal Opportunities Unit

Trevor Carter talking to Sarah Olowe

Trevor Carter began teaching in 1972 at Brookhouse Boys' School in Hackney and was appointed Head of the ILEA's Equal Opportunities Unit in 1989. He has been an executive member of the National Union of Teachers and was a founding member of the Caribbean Teachers' Association and the National Convention of Black Teachers.

In 1975 I went to the USA with a team of educationalists led by Peter Newsam, the then Deputy Education Officer. It was on that trip, whilst looking at schools in New York, that the whole idea of a multi-ethnic policy evolved. The experience was horrible. New York schools, particularly the schools we saw in the Bronx, were remarkable because everything was going on in them except education. Traditional New York manufacturers were moving out of the USA to get away from high wages and going to Latin America, Colombia and Panama, where they could get cheap labour. This meant that over fifty percent of black people were unemployed. I don't want to go overboard and say London is like that, but I think we learnt. We learnt what not to do and we came back.

If there is unemployment in an area certain things will happen: the level of alcohol abuse and drug-taking will increase and families will become insecure. When children are not enthusiastic in school and the community is not supporting them, then teachers reflect that frustration.

In New York, the authorities were not successful in recruiting sufficient black teachers. There was a teachers' strike in 1968 when people demanded that services be decentralised. One of the community's demands was that it should hire and fire teachers and administrators. The teachers objected, and it meant that for the first time there was a serious conflict between Jewish and black people. The teaching union, mainly made up of white Jews, was on strike and picketing schools, while the people breaking the strike were black. There were some very nasty confrontations. We decided that a similar situation must not be allowed to happen here and so the ILEA's first policy on multi-ethnic education was produced. It was unanimously agreed by Members of all political parties. At that time we had one inspector, Bev Woodroffe, responsible for something roughly corresponding to anti-racist education; it was his initiative which created the large team of multi-cultural or anti-racist educationalists within the Authority.

The other aspect of my participation and work in education was the formation of the Caribbean Teachers' Association. Peter Newsam quickly accepted our request for consultation and that opened an extremely positive ambience in the Authority. Under his guidance we were able to develop policies without the kinds of conflicts that were found in other authorities and organisations at the time. I would like to think that the whole idea of consultation within the Authority came out of those days when the leadership of the Caribbean Teachers' Association sat with the ILEA's senior officers and took important issues like supplementary schools, expulsions and the need for black teachers and simply discussed them. It was through these sessions that many senior and middle-ranking officers became sensitive to the issues, and we were able to help them understand what racism and oppression are all about. One very senior officer told me quite recently that while he was widely read on racism he only really learnt about the pain of being oppressed through personal contact with black people. I think that this is the kind of sensitivity that we encouraged. In the early years, many activists were absorbed into the system. But being absorbed has softened our impact; we defend the institution because we are part of it.

I think that nearly all the black organisations that were dominated by those of us born in the West Indies have become stale. We have not been able to identify sufficiently with what I call the black British. Young people see us as old fogeys. They tolerate us, but that is all. We have not been able to identify sufficiently with them either intellectually or culturally. For example, there are still many, many black people who do not understand what the Rastafarian Movement is.

In this society it is traditionally the middle classes who have got the time and the know-how to struggle and to attempt to reform situations. But too few of us give up some of our weekends to give our skills back to the community. If you go around to all the basic organisations, particularly the supplementary schools, in ninety-nine percent of cases you'll find a woman, a sort of black mother earth, running the thing. Around her you will have a few young people, probably first-year teachers. They use that experience to get ahead but they don't look back. Very few conscientiously say: 'Look, the higher I go, the longer life becomes.' I believe the only way we can recreate ourselves is if we make it a point of duty to give some time regularly, rather like going to church. Another thing which saddens me in this respect is seeing teachers who call themselves professional belittle working-class women who, often without any formal qualifications, set up community education projects. I have seen some young teachers embarrassed by these people, who could be their parents, because of the way they speak, dress and act. The organiser then becomes self-conscious and starts to lose confidence when, in fact, they are the spirit around which the place revolves.

Many Caribbean Teachers' Association members currently run supplementary schools in an organisation called the Robert Hart Memorial School, which was founded in 1972. There is a constant struggle within the organisation between those people who want to apply for grants and those who do not. I have been one of the latter. I sincerely feel that people appreciate much more the things they create themselves. The ILEA has freely recognised the role of supplementary schools and has attempted to support them, but bureaucracies tend to absorb projects once they start giving them money.

There are still not enough black teachers, and certainly not enough black heads, but that is because of the problem education *per se* is facing. The job is difficult; add the racial dimension and you have our current situation. I would like to think, because I am Head of Equal Opportunities, that the Authority has devised criteria which make the selection process much fairer, but it isn't working. All sorts of scallywags simply learn the words and do good interviews.

The now defunct Ethnic Minorities Section lasted for three years, until 1986. The Committee members comprised of two black delegates from each division, elected by community organisations interested in education. Its job was to oversee most of the committee reports produced by the ILEA. For the first time officers recognised that, when policies which affected black people were being drafted, it made sense to have black voices in that process. It was chaos sometimes because many people were inexperienced, but the recognition by the ILEA that Londoners are not all the same marked an important step forward.

The ILEA is being abolished, in part, because it went on to create the Equal Opportunities Unit and anti-racist policies. Although many minority ethnic people, gay and lesbian people and women have pooh-poohed the Unit, those who are against progress and reform took it seriously and abolished the whole Authority because of it. When the ILEA was thinking of setting up the unit some people argued that equal opportunities should instead be spread through the whole Authority and that there should not be a special section of the Authority responsible for it. I disagreed because I believed that an organisation that is historically white and racist needed a catalyst to make the policies work. Many of the officers, efficient and good as they were, did not understand what equal opportunities are about. I could not blame them for not understanding it. They are not black people. If any one of us had worked in the same way for twenty-five years *we* would have difficulty changing.

The problem with something like the Equal Opportunities Unit, however, is that sometimes you lose your way. You start writing articles, making speeches and not really working towards what you were set up to achieve. People in the organisation make demands on you. Committees demand that you do certain kinds of things and the politicians demand that you do certain kinds of things; sometimes those things are nonsense.

The Equal Opportunities Unit was there to make sure that the policies of the ILEA were carried out by all the senior officers and to make sure that anti-racism and multi-culturalism became part of education rather than something slapped on its backside. Good education must, by definition, be anti-racist. I am not sure we succeeded. For some people, advocating equal opportunities has become a method of holding on to a senior job.

The teaching profession understands much more than it did before, but the figures that we have got from our statistics branch show that Afro-Caribbean kids are still expelled more often than the children of any other ethnic group. Statistics also show that black people are more prone to schizophrenia. There is a link between oppression, the filling of jails and expulsions from schools. Teachers, educational psychologists, dinner ladies, everybody contributes to this. These kids are not usually mad or crazy but it has taken conventional wisdom a long time to accept that the black family is not the problem. It is only now that researchers and statisticians are putting the blame on the institution.

One of the problems with bureaucracy and society generally is that, although they might not deliberately go out to assimilate people, they usually promote those who look like or sound like them. Many of us were fooled by that. We need to learn the skill of being double-cultured. I come from a background which was influenced considerably by the Black Movement struggles. I was educated in the West Indies by poorly-paid teachers who were badly treated and lacked resources; but they were educated people who could use racist books to teach you about yourself and could use the Bible to teach history and politics. In my early days at home, before the civil rights struggles, teachers were the only models I had to respect. You could not respect policemen, and you certainly could not respect civil servants because they were the people on the other side of the counter trying not to give you what was yours. So in a way teaching was a moral thing to do. I was also a romantic.

Prior to the early eighties, when I was in the thick of things, of the eighty-nine members of staff at my school I was the only person who had a Caribbean background. There were meetings, conferences, marches, parents and governors to organise. Because of my activities I was invited to apply for a fellowship at the Institute of Education. I got it, and while I was there I was head-hunted for a job here as a Senior Education Liaison Officer. I can remember the drama of being chosen. It was not easy to resist. Teaching is a hell of a job, but you get so tired without realising it. Once you leave, the school and kids start to recede into the distance. But come abolition there is a possibility that, if I am still brave, I will go back to teaching.

The new Education Reform Act, which is responsible for abolishing the ILEA, has created a problem for its perpetrators. Destroying the Authority was intended to create a climate where reformers were stifled. They have another thing coming. Black people are crucial in the inner city areas and, although some of us may not have recognised it yet, the government has put power in our hands.

An Assistant Education Officer

Gus John talking to Sarah Olowe

Gus John joined the ILEA in 1987 as Assistant Education Officer (Community Education) after having worked in the education service in Manchester. In 1989 he became Chief Education Officer for the London Borough of Hackney.

I was attracted to the ILEA because I had a view of it as an innovative education authority. I come from a community-education background and had retained a keen interest in what was going on in adult education and the Youth Service. The way in which the ILEA Adult Education Service went about securing opportunities for adults was quite impressive. The Manchester service was much less well organised. It did not have as high a profile, and in many ways there was too much wrangling, largely because there were very powerful further education principals who were concerned to preserve their courses, irrespective of their value to the public. We used to have some pretty dreadful community education management team meetings where these principals would preen themselves and generally behave like schoolboys. The whole thing became very, very tedious indeed. Then I came to the ILEA.

One of the things that struck me like a thunderbolt was the fact that the Authority, which presented a unified and purposeful view of itself externally, had a structure that I frankly found unbelievable. The ILEA was supposed to be a unitary authority providing education in some kind of coherent manner, but the lack of uniformity of approach between the various phases of the education system was quite incredible. There was the Further Education Section, the Community Section and the Careers Section. Apart from management team meetings once a week, these sections did not talk to one another. There were very rigid structures geared to the advancement and preservation of each particular sector. The structures did not seem to have either the clients' needs or the most appropriate ways of delivering services to them in mind.

There was some excellent work going on in community education projects based on school campuses: in George Green, Islington; in Waterfield, Tower Hamlets; in Lilian Baylis, Greenwich and so on. They were set up as experimental projects around 1981-82, but there was very little evidence of the results of any of them being allowed to have any value in a wider sense. It was not possible to detect a rational and systematic purpose behind making these things happen. I believe there is plenty of room for experimental projects to act as measures of the appropriateness of the non-experimental and more routine mainstream activity. Nevertheless, these projects did provide opportunities for those taking part to gain very valuable experience and improve their own practice as individuals.

The voluntary sector, with which the ILEA worked in partnership, gave rise to some quite innovative projects and developments, especially in the area of equal opportunities: work with disabled people, work with women and work with young black people. One of the things that I found slightly difficult about all of this was that while the ILEA was concerned about being responsive to the communities and their requirements externally – resulting in courses being planned around the needs of black people, and in some instances in the recruitment of more black people, particularly at middle and junior levels – it was not very good at ensuring that the white power structures within the Authority itself were adequately challenged. It had all the policy statements on equal opportunities, race and gender, yet right in the belly of County Hall there was the Multi-Cultural Inspectorate, led by Michael Hussey, which, structurally speaking, was totally marginalised. It consisted almost exclusively of black people, but it seems there was no mechanism for the work they did to affect the rest of the Authority.

Some twelve or thirteen years ago an organisation came into being called the Afro-Caribbean Education Resource Centre (ACER). It did work around issues of curriculum and, in particular, drew on the experiences of black people in this country to generate curricula that could be used in schools. It produced excellent publications, many of which were printed by the ILEA Learning Resources Branch and, over the years, teachers and educational authorities in other parts of the country ordered material from ACER for use in their own curriculum development and teaching. The staff at ACER did a lot of work training teachers, but it was almost impossible for its team of workers (ultimately managed by Mike Hussey as the Senior Inspector within the Multi-Cultural Inspectorate) to get their inspector colleagues with subject responsibilities in English, history, social studies, geography and so on to take the products of ACER's work seriously and disseminate them within the mainstream subject areas.

My understanding is that Mike Hussey and friends of ACER created space for developments, but there was not the will from the Chief Inspector for the Authority as a whole, or from the officers in the Schools Branch, to ensure that anything actually happened. Although ACER was mainly a schools-focused project, they received much more support from the Community Education Sector in the ILEA. The Authority seemed content to boast that it had ten members of staff in ACER even though they were funded through Section 11. (Section 11 of the Local Government Act of 1966 enables local authorities to apply to the government for extra funding for projects which could be said to benefit people of Commonwealth origin and their descendants.)

The Centre for Urban Educational Studies (CUES) was treated in an almost identical fashion. The Centre did a lot of pioneering work, particularly in the seventies when the Authority did not have a Multi-Cultural Inspectorate or teachers' centres concentrating on issues to do with multi-cultural education and anti-racist education was virtually unheard of. CUES continued to do things that were extremely relevant throughout the eighties; but, although it had the capacity, it did not become a centre of excellence for the theoretical and practical development of mainstream education issues.

To put it bluntly, quite a number of the senior officers in the

ILEA were committed to doing things simply because they were the flavour of the month. They liked the idea of the ILEA being seen as the trailblazer and, in many respects, that remained the only motivating force. There was no commitment to improving the life chances of black people.

That was a long-winded and intelligent way of saying that there was a hell of a lot of bloody racism within that damned place. The ILEA is effectively a white power structure; and the fact that, after the abolition of the GLC, more black people joined them, the fact that they came to have a significant number of black elected Members in the Authority, was not sufficient to turn around the racist culture on which that place had thrived for decades. Herman Ouseley's appointment as Chief Executive was politically very significant, but that was one man, using all his wits to prevent himself being undermined by others at a similar level to himself. And some of them treated him pretty disgracefully, I have to say.

At my very first meeting, when I addressed all the Adult Education Institute principals in the ILEA, I was the only black person present in a room with twenty-six people in it. The majority of students served by those institutes are black, but at one stage the ILEA could boast only two black vice-principals. After a massive battle I managed to appoint another; she later became the principal of the Clapham-Battersea Adult Education Institute. The ILEA relied almost exclusively on white people to fill its positions of power, however much it professed anti-racism.

It is a bleak picture. Apart from Bebb Burchell, who became Senior Education Officer for Equal Opportunities, Herman Ouseley and myself were the only black managers at that level of the organisation. A lot was demanded of us. There was an expectation that you would subscribe to County Hall culture and maintain a hands-off approach in matters which, in other people's perceptions, did not concern you. What the officers did not understand is that racism does not respect those particular boundaries, nor should those who are the victims of racism be expected to respect those particular boundaries.

I regularly had people coming to see me; I was not their line manager, but they knew I had a particular profile in terms of my politics, former management jobs and role within the community. For many of them, having me and Herman Ouseley in that place was a kind of lifeline. They would come and register particular grievances, share concerns, and request our intervention in matters that were particularly weighty. They were effectively doing two things: recognising our role at a certain level within the institution, and the power it was presumed to give us; and, at the same time, using us as a sort of sounding board. If they did not require us to intervene directly they wanted to use our experience and expertise to plan their own action.

This did not go down particularly well with other managers because they believed that the integrity of their own offices was paramount, and that senior managers should not break rank. I do not think that many people understand the challenges or dilemmas of the black professional person in these kinds of bureaucracies. The system of redressing grievances took the pain and hurt of black people and, almost inevitably, reduced it to some kind of bureaucratic procedure.

People were constantly being passed over when they applied for senior posts, largely because a particular inspector did not like their politics, did not like the look of their face, or thought they were not deferential or obsequious enough. Particularly, distressing was that when both circumstantial and incontrovertible evidence of discrimination within the organisation was presented to senior managers, those managers preferred to allow the aggrieved individuals to suffer the hurt and injustice rather than challenge those responsible. Perhaps they were unable to deal with the fact that, if managers could be discriminating in those kinds of ways, they ought not to have been in those positions of power.

I found it pretty galling.

A Graduate Recruit

Veron Strachan

Veron Strachan joined the ILEA in 1983 through the Graduate Recruitment Scheme. She went on to work in a variety of departments, including Research and Statistics and the Corporate Support Team. In 1989 Ms Strachan became the Education Co-Ordinator for the London Borough of Lambeth.

Any black person working for the ILEA and trying to assess the experience will almost certainly have mixed feelings. It is definitely a case of "could do better"; but on the other hand it could have been worse!

I say this because, in a sense, I have taken for granted an ethos that was developed in the Authority after years of debate on how to create and implement a policy of equal opportunities for all. Certain discussions have taken place and people have generally moved on to more sophisticated concepts of equality and what is needed to achieve it.

At a meeting about life after the ILEA, a Member of another education authority was asked to say why the top two tiers of their education department contained no officers from black and ethnic minorities. His response was wholly negative in tone, with statements such as 'black candidates don't apply', and he informed those present of the terrible consequences of tokenism. In other words, it was the fault of the black community, not the council. I felt that we had had this kind of discussion in the ILEA some time ago, and had decided that discrimination did have something to do with it. I am certain that in some parts of the

Authority such comments are still made; but it still came as a shock to hear this kind of statement from a politician.

I was recruited to the Authority through an "elite" process called the Graduate Recruitment scheme, which ceased some time ago. The people on the scheme were expected to go on to occupy the higher echelons of the Authority. I was the only black candidate in my year. My career was reasonably successful and happy, but frustration with the bureaucracy of the Authority was my overriding experience.

My main interest is the education of black pupils, particularly Afro-Caribbean pupils. It is something of an obsession with me, and everybody expects me to get on my soapbox whenever the subject is raised. I am very simplistic in my views, deliberately so, because I think that too many people cloud the issues with complex theorising about cause and effect. Perhaps a list of my favourite statements will serve to illustrate my platform. No doubt people will dismantle it from time to time!

– Teachers are *not* social workers. Their attention must be clearly focused on the fact that their main role is to educate.

– Achievement, as measured by examination results, test results, careers and so on, is absolutely crucial and should be the main yardstick by which success in education is measured. Although there are other measures, these are the kinds of currency that count in this society, and these are the outcomes that black parents want when they send their children to school.

– There must be more black officers, teachers, Members, parents and so on, in every part of the education service. You don't need meetings to consult them separately if they are an integral part of the service.

I have been taking a keen interest in recent research which seems to demonstrate that schools can make a difference to achievement. I have always felt this instinctively, and I am simply not prepared to accept that racism and deprivation inevitably lead to failure in relation to education.

Year after year I have been disappointed that, despite all the efforts of the Authority, black children continue to underachieve. However, I detect a sea change in the approach to tackling this. Research seems to show that there can be success in the face of all kinds of factors which prevent black pupils and students from achieving their full potential. Time and time again I have come across ex-ILEA pupils who have used their own initiative and resources to obtain the education and qualifications which they should have obtained at school. I feel that this resourcefulness will be our salvation. I am equally pleased to see the increasing number of black parents, students and professionals who are seeking active involvement in the running of schools and colleges and are able to articulate their views and concerns.

In the future, I hope, Members and officers will not have to spend a lot of time trying to imagine what the concerns of the black community might be and they won't have to call special meetings to discuss them. Black people will be present within the structures that make and implement policies, and there will be no need to seek their views after decisions are made. I am optimistic that in a few years' time this will be very much the case. Black people are no longer waiting for the gate to the secret garden to be opened for them – they are opening the gate themselves.

Multi-Ethnic and Anti-Racist Inspector 1

Ranjit Dheer talking to Sarah Olowe

Ranjit Dheer taught in ILEA schools from 1970 to 1982, when he became an inspector. He is currently Assistant Director of Education for the London Borough of Southwark.

Who do you see, almost every day, outside teacher's study? A black child. Who do you see being assaulted in the playground? Who do you see in the lowest stream at school?

The Afro-Caribbean child is generally regarded as aggressive, unacademic, sports-minded, gregarious and minded to challenge authority. They are expected to come into conflict with the school hierarchy: teachers, dinner ladies, schoolkeepers, headteachers and laboratory assistants. At the most serious level, you find them being referred to the educational psychologist because they are seen to be giving problems and being disruptive. They then get placed in units for children who have behavioural problems.

Asian children are viewed differently. They are withdrawn, obedient, do not cause trouble, are prepared to take instructions and unlikely to challenge. They are at the opposite end of the spectrum from the Afro-Caribbean child. Pupils are seen in these ways because those who assess the two groups of children have a culturally specific view of what a child should be within a particular education system – the English education system – and neither of these stereotypes fits into it. The Afro-Caribbean child is labelled as disruptive and a potential troublemaker; the Asian child is perceived in a different way, but seen as equally problematic.

Discrimination now takes subtle forms. It does not present itself in the crude forms that we saw as teachers in the sixties and seventies. Basically, what it means is that black children do not have an equal chance in schools. This has been proved by a large volume of literature, reports and documents published in the last thirty years. There is racism in the curriculum, in the way black teachers are treated; there is racism in the way languages are taught in schools, there is racism in the way black children are harassed, there is racism in the way cleaners are always black and teachers are usually white. The curriculum is not broad enough to include the experience of the black child. If you analyse the content of what is taught in schools – in English, history, social studies, geography, maths, science – it is quite clear that the content of what is taught is from a racist, white perspective.

English teachers are very proud of the fact that English schools are child-centred. When the child comes to school, the teachers and the assistants value the experiences of the child and what that child brings in terms of culture, language and lifestyle. This is a good thing, but it does not happen in the case of the black child. When the black child crosses the threshold of the school it means a break with home. This is why large numbers of black children suffer from some kind of break or blockage; they suffer psychologically. As a teacher it really worries me. A white mother of a mixed race child recently described how her six-year-old daughter burst into tears and, scratching her chest, explained that she did not like her new dress because it resulted in 'too much rubbishy brown showing'. I think we seriously underestimate the ability of children to instinctively understand what is going on around them.

I trained as a teacher in 1969 at Bristol University. Later on I did a Master's degree in Education. I became an inspector seventeen years after I began teaching. I would like to think that I was employed because I had the necessary skills and I met the selection criteria, but a lot of teachers have been denied promotion deliberately. There are teachers – I know dozens of them – who have left teaching because of it. They get left behind because they don't get nominated for management roles. The black candidate does not get sent on management courses, so at interviews they are at a disadvantage. When the headship of a school falls vacant, the inspectors have the authority to put somebody in that post on a temporary basis. It is ninety-nine percent likely that a white candidate will be placed as acting head and allowed to get, for example, six months' experience. At the end of six months it is very difficult to reject that candidate.

The Authority employs 93,000 staff from the cleaners to the Chief Executive. The black population in inner London schools and institutions is about fifty percent. Yet the number of black teachers within the ILEA is only five percent. Out of nearly 850 secondary schools the number of black headteachers can be counted on the fingers of two hands! Similarly with officers, out of a total force of 165 inspectors there are only fifteen black people. In the senior rungs of the inspectorate you find fewer and fewer black inspectors; of the fifteen, most are lower-scale inspectors like myself.

Inspectors are responsible for monitoring the implementation of the curriculum in schools; that is, monitoring what is taught. We are also extensively involved in appointing teachers, headteachers and ancillary teachers. Although no inspector will ever admit it, we have a great deal of power. The ILEA is a democratically elected body and as such it can vote in a policy, but the implementation of the policy is done by the officers. Sadly, parts of the inspectorate have been very, very obstructive. A lot of good work that could have been done has been weakened by senior officers. For example, black teachers who are working for the implementation of anti-racist policies have often had their promotions blocked.

At a theoretical level, the ILEA has the best policies in the country. But progress has been slow because the Authority assumed that the senior officers and inspectors did not need in-service training. In other words, it was assumed that officers were on the side of anti-racism and that the real work needed to be done in schools. In fact, my experience is that the real advances have been made by schools and teachers locally. Teachers have done a tremendous amount of work. They have raised their own awareness a great deal, begun to make links with the communities and looked for newer, less racist materials.

It is senior officers who have not been as helpful as they could have been.

Multi-Ethnic and Anti-Racist Inspector 2

Leela Ramdeen

Haringey's Assistant Chief Education Officer, Leela Ramdeen, was Multi-Ethnic and Anti-Racist Inspector for the ILEA from 1986 to 1988.

'W*ell done, young lady, on your appointment as an inspector – for London Transport?'* These words still ring in my ears as I reflect on my experiences as an Inspector for Multi-ethnic and Anti-racist Education in the ILEA. The words were supposed to have been congratulatory, and were uttered by a renowned white male on hearing of my appointment. I suppose that it is what one would refer to as unintentional racism. A similar comment was made in November 1989 by a popular sports commentator who told the public that it was fortunate for Britain that the Trinidad and Tobago football team did not win their World Cup qualifier against the USA for the final in Italy. If Trinidad and Tobago had won, he reasoned, the whole of London Transport would have ground to a halt.

Like so many other local education authorities, the huge bureaucracy of the ILEA sought to change institutional and personal forms of discrimination by appointing a number of specialist teams in the hope that these teams would effect change across the Authority. The publication of the race, sex and class documents by the ILEA in the mid 1970s was the culmination of years of struggle by black and ethnic minority groups and committed white people in the Authority. There was, however, no overall corporate strategy.

What was needed was strategic planning and implementation which involved all partners in the education process. Unless there was total commitment to, and ownership of, the issues, any plan would flounder. But this required the right climate. I believe that it was necessary to create a climate of success from the grass roots upwards, and from the pinnacle of the hierarchy down. From the point of view of the hierarachy in the Authority, there were a number of elected Members from black and ethnic minority groups who could have had more impact if they had caucused effectively. At officer/inspector level there were problems because of the fragmentation of the various groups that were established to promote equal opportunities. The teams which focused on gender equality, race equality and bilingualism and community languages worked, in the main, separately from the rest of County Hall – a vast institution. This arrangement did not facilitate collaborative working. The opportunities which were created and developed depended on goodwill for any results rather than on structured planning, monitoring and evaluation.

A constant complaint of the advisory teachers and lecturers who worked with the team of inspectors for multi-ethnic and anti racist education was that the work was marginalised. When collaborative work between various advisory teachers and inspectors worked well one celebrated, and hoped that the good practice would permeate the entire education process. It didn't help matters that the status of the inspectors for multi-ethnic and anti-racist education was relatively low. We would have had more clout in such a highly hierarchical structure if we had been at a more senior level. Attempting to influence the practice of senior colleagues as a basic grade inspector was difficult.

From a personal point of view, I soon recognised the need for an individual plan of action which would inadvertently affect the work of others. My responsibility within the team of five was for the primary schools across the Authority. I also had specific responsibility for promoting race equality across all ages in Hammersmith and Fulham and Kensington and Chelsea, Camden and Westminster.

Having worked as the co-ordinator for a post-Rampton project in the ILEA (the Primary Curriculum Development Project for pupils of Caribbean origin), I had developed feel for the development process in the primary sector. I was supported to a great extent by the fact that the Chief Inspector, David Hargreaves, had developed his understanding of the issues by listening to criticisms of his report, *Improving Secondary Schools,* (ISS) and by considering seriously the findings of documents such as the ILEA *Junior School Project Report* which highlighted the fact that black pupils, particularly boys of Caribbean origin, were denied appropriate educational provision.

The Primary School Staff Inspector, Barbara MacGilchrist, accepted my argument that in order to influence the primary sector I needed to be seen as part of the education team. I am still bemused, however, by the fact that it took six months before my name appeared in an appropriate manner on the minutes of monthly meetings. For six months I was included under the heading 'OTHER'.

In areas where I was able to have some influence I often felt that I was walking a tightrope. For example, as a member of the working group on parental involvement I was able to put forward the views of various client groups about deficiencies in the ILEA's service provision. Another small step was taken when printed guidelines on parental involvement were produced. However, the community saw me as a member of the establishment and felt I should be affecting change more swiftly. I understood their frustration, but had to learn to bear the brunt of their complaints.

It is difficult to evaluate precisely what impact our work had on the teaching and learning process in the Authority, but our work on equal opportunities became known nationally and internationally. Across the ILEA, seminars, conferences and workshops were organised, and the materials produced by groups working on these teams were promoted and sold. All this made an invaluable contribution in raising awareness of the issues. However, the publication of examination results in the mid-eighties showed that the Authority was still failing to meet the educational needs of significant numbers of students from black and ethnic minority groups. Analysis of statistical data seemed to give the impression that the Asian students were performing better, but this impression was deceptive, particularly as we knew we were failing to meet the educational needs of great numbers of working-class students of Bangladeshi origin in areas like Tower Hamlets.

One characteristic of black inspectors in the ILEA was "staying power". We developed mutual support through caucusing. Looking back on the dinners that we had together, and the meetings to discuss issues relating to black teachers, headteachers, students and so on, I realise how important these sessions were. It is not that we weren't involved with our white colleagues, collaborative working with others was essential, but it was also important to share ideas with black workers who were experiencing similar difficulties in various parts of the Authority. At our meetings, tension was released as joked and laughed, almost in a nervous way, about issues that had serious implications for the achievement of all learners. By releasing tension we were able to free ourselves for a while from the struggle of trying to bring about change in a huge bureaucracy. Indeed, the very centre of this bureaucracy, County Hall, beautiful as it is, reeks of the effects of colonialism. The drip, drip, dripping of change was mainly imperceptible.

I remember how frustrated the black Science Inspector became when colleagues in the inspectorate and the rest of the field constantly asked him if he was a new multi-ethnic or anti-racist worker. Indeed, for a number of years appointments of inspectors from black and ethnic minority groups were made mainly to the team of inspectors for multi-ethnic and anti-racist education and the team for bilingualism and community languages. The log jam of black professionals dispersed with the news of the abolition of the ILEA. Many black colleagues applied for jobs in the thirteen boroughs, and a significant proportion of these individuals were appointed to senior positions. The Science Inspector is now a Deputy Director in one of the London boroughs.

The various black teachers' groups across the Authority developed strength over the years, and their struggles led to two major conferences at County Hall. These conferences focused specifically on their plight and gave them an opportunity to seek redress for various injustices within the system relating to their position and status. In 1987 David Hargreaves established regular meetings with inspectors from black and ethnic minority groups. This forum provided an opportunity for colleagues to express issues which we had grown accustomed to discussing among ourselves. Mr. Hargreaves hosted the first black headteachers' conference in the ILEA, and it was there that the extent and nature of racism in the educational system was made clear. I found it overwhelming to hear lengthy and painful accounts of the obstacles that lay in the path of these talented black teachers; individuals whose journeys to headship were littered with examples of institutional and personal racism. This conference led to the formation of a black headteacher and deputy headteacher association which has grown from strength to strength.

The meetings between David Hargreaves and inspectors from black and ethnic minority groups led to the establishment of a task group to devise strategies to promote race equality for black teachers. A comprehensive strategy was about to be launched when the abolition of the ILEA was announced.

More and more supplementary schools were opened within the ILEA during my service and I often found myself at conferences and community meetings trying to convince members of these communities that they should continue to struggle for their rights within the mainstream. So committed was I to making curriculum entitlement a reality for all learners that I was often stunned by the anger of parents who had had enough of the rhetoric from educationalists, who failed to deliver quality education appropriate to the needs, interests, and entitlements of black children.'How many generations must we lose before people like you realise that the only way forward is to open our own schools?' said one mother to me. Disillusionment! Frustration! Anger! Schools such as John Loughborough were on the tongues of many who felt that the state system had failed. Black governors formed collectives across the Authority and many sought to influence educational practice by putting themselves forward for appointment as governors bodies. However, some of the people who were appointed as governors found that they were marginalised and because of inadequate training were unable to cue in to a system that seemed to deliberately mystify the education process.

It is important to contextualise the struggle for race equality within the national context. Each annual report from the CRE highlights the fact that generally there has not been the will on the part of society at large to eradicate racism. On the contrary, research showed that it was on the increase. The fact that quality and equality are inextricably linked seems to have become lost in a squabble between the far left and the far right.

There are many who believe that Stuart MacLure's analysis in *Education Reform* is correct, and that the government is determined to bring about major changes, using the Education Reform Act in order to curb the anti-racist movement. Personally, I think that many aspects of the new Act will be beneficial, but others, such as 'temporary exceptions' (school suspensions) could adversely affect black and ethnic minority students.

I hope that the thirteen new authorities presently being formed will not put equal opportunities on back burner but will ensure that priniciples of equality will be embedded in their development plans. If educationalists in the state sector do not get their act together then various community groups will act by using their feet, and send their children to private schools or to black community schools. We all need to take heed of their concerns and to act in a responsible manner to gain credibility in the eyes of the communities that we serve.

At the end of the day all parents want, is for their children to have access to an education that would enable them to enter society as competent, confident, self-reliant individuals. What they do not want is for their children to leave school and college with records of achievement that are biased and based on stereotypical views of their capabilities. It still seems strange to me that one should have to battle for students' entitlement in an education system that claims it is concerned to promote equality of access and opportunity for all.

Multi-Ethnic and Anti-Racist Inspector 3

Sukhdev Singh

Sukhdev Singh is the Assistant Director of Education for the London Borough of Tower Hamlets. From 1979 until the beginning of July 1989 he was Multi-Ethnic Education Inspector at the ILEA.

I joined the ILEA as an Inspector for Multi-Ethnic Education (MEE) in September 1979 with a specific brief for the post-school sector covering further, higher and community education. At that time there was very little MEE outside the schools sector in terms of policy or service delivery. I started with an almost blank sheet.

For induction purposes I was attached for a period of one week to the relatively progressive principal of North London College, who had recognised the importance of MEE quite early and was attempting to develop a policy. It soon became abundantly clear that the progress towards multi-ethnic and anti-racist education in the further education sector was going to be painfully slow, and my purpose was to speed up that process to a level where it would take off and become self-sustaining.

Almost the first task – apart from understanding the complexities of the ILEA's structures and its institutions – was to identify potential growth points. To do this it was necessary to discover allies, opponents and other obstacles, both real and imaginary. Prior to my arrival, the ILEA had given authority to appoint two advisory lecturers to support my work.

Unfortunately, the Committee Report had not included any provision for accommodation or office furniture. Therefore, after appointing them, I spent a great deal of time negotiating a base for them and getting telephones and filing cabinets and so on. This process taught me the absolute necessity of writing well-planned reports which take account of the practical, as well as the theoretical, aspects of policy implementation.

As my post was formally located within the schools sector I was heavily drawn into the programme of school visits, inspections and so on, as well as having specific responsibility for MEE in Wandsworth. I tended to concentrate on secondary schools but was also involved in work through the Authority. This caused some tensions between myself and other members of the team, who naturally saw the schools as the major focus of their work. Despite this, we maintained respect and affection between all members of the team, whatever their individual points of view. We were, at least, all working towards the same end.

The arrangement and status of Multi-Ethnic Inspectors also caused some difficulties. Initially, inspectorate colleagues in the further, higher and community education teams did not recognise me as one of their number. By 1983 I was still being paid at the lower rate (SO6) rather than at the district inspector rate (SO4). I felt like an honorary district inspector – responsibility without monetary reward. However, I was made an acting SO4 in 1984 after being appointed as the Chief Inspector's personal representative with responsibility for teachers' grievances.

It was important for me to devise a set of strategies which were likely to succeed and which were based on my own knowledge and beliefs. Right from the start I had an integrationist approach; I strongly believed that in order for MEE to succeed and have a lasting impact it had to be knitted into the fabric of the educational system and be part of mainstream education. It could not be bolted on or be regarded as an optional extra. Nor did I believe that multi-ethnic initiatives could be seen as a passing fad which would disappear in due course. Out of this belief, and the fact that racism is endemic in society as a whole, it was vital that powerful individuals in the ILEA, such as college principals, inspectors and education officers, were influenced. Their levels of awareness had to be raised so that the issues relating to ethnic minority communities remained high on their personal, and hidden, agendas. The main issues were obstacles to educational achievement such as restricted access and opportunity due to racial discrimination or a lack of understanding of the special needs of minority groups. Also important was the longer-term goal of multi-cultural education for all students.

With the help of the two advisory lecturers, I wrote comprehensive guidelines for the promotion of MEE in colleges of further and higher education. After numerous discussions and consultations with bodies such as the Commission for Racial Equality and the National Association of Teachers of Further and Higher Education, we published *Guidelines on MEE for Colleges.* This document was monitored by the Chief Inspector of Further and Higher Community Education (FHCE) and had his full support. It included guidance on policy, staffing, curriculum, racism, languages and so on. A key recommendation was the appointment in each college of a Multi-Ethnic Education Senior Lecturer (MEESL). This was considered too radical a proposal by some inspectors and there was also considerable opposition from the Association of Principals and Vice-Principals. However, after a tortuous round of negotiations, the ILEA Education Committee authorised these appointments.

The reasoning behind the creation of these posts was both subtle and complex. Firstly, I saw this as an opportunity to recruit some black staff at a level where they were otherwise grossly underrepresented, and to use it as a bridge which could provide a route to more senior posts.

Secondly, I wanted these posts firmly based and rooted in colleges. I did not wish these postholders to become merely liaison officers who had trouble-shooting functions; the objective was to make them active agents of change. There was pressure from my colleagues to create these posts as advisory co-ordinators who would report directly to me rather than to the senior management in the colleges (cf the schools model of Divisional Multi-Ethnic Co-Ordinators).

Thirdly, I strongly believe that change occurs by working with people from the inside and, therefore, I built in a definite teaching role. MEESLs were required to devote half of their time to teaching a specialist subject in order to enhance their credibility among lecturing staff.

Fourthly, it was important to demonstrate that this initiative was cost-effective and excellent value for money. By this means I was able to create a team of twenty-two MEESLs at a net additional cost to the ILEA equivalent to just under three senior lecturers. This was achieved by obtaining funds from the Home Office under Section 11 of the Local Government Act of 1966. The somewhat uncertain nature of Section 11 funding was the other reason why I did not want to base these posts outside educational institutions.

Lastly, I was concerned to maintain flexibility in the system to allow career development opportunities for MEESLs so that they did not become trapped in a multi-ethnic cul-de-sac.

Much time was spent on this enterprise and I carried out my own, unofficial, ethnic monitoring while these appointments were being made. I was concerned to ensure that no gender or ethnic group should feel excluded. It is for others to judge the success of this operation. What is undeniable is that a number of MEESLs very quickly gained promotion to senior posts such as vice-principal, principal and inspector.

As for other areas in the post-school sector, a similar approach was adopted as in adult education. Guidelines were written and posts with responsibility for MEE were created. Emphasis was on providing greater access for students and more training opportunities for tutors. In the Youth Service most of the work was done by the appropriate inspectors. However, progress was made from with in the Youth Service and a number of black staff were appointed. Some work was done by advising inspectors and work experience co-ordinators in the careers service, and the cross-curriculum nature of careers work made it easier for them to appreciate the style and methodology of MEE. They were included in the various training courses and conferences organise by the multi-ethnic team.

The development and implementation of an MEE policy in the post-school sector was significantly different from that in schools. In the latter the politicians and political processes played a greater role. The other major difference was that, particularly in further education, developments were focused in the educational establishments rather than in County Hall. On the other hand, specific guidelines were introduced into the post-school sector from the centre at a time when such prescriptive guidance of schools would have been considered outrageous. Despite the fact that I deliberately adopted a low-key approach to my work, at the time many people regarded the post-school initiative as revolutionary.

Servicing Staff

View from the Shop 1

Mabel Headley talking to Sarah Olowe

Mabel Headley has been Assistant Manager and Cashier at County Hall's general store for fourteen years.

To begin with we just sold snacks, you know, sweets and pies and things, but recently the shop went big-scale and has become a little supermarket. It is the only shop in County Hall so everyone passes through here. Now and again you get a customer that is a bit grumpy – probably because their work is getting them down – but it doesn't last for long. They usually come back the next day and apologise for being angry.

I have five children. Three of them joined me from Barbados and two were born here. They all went to ILEA schools in Wandsworth where I was impressed with the standard of education. My last daughter has finished now but she came out having done very well. She got a diploma in business studies and is now working in the word processing department somewhere upstairs. Sometimes she comes to see me at the shop. Junior is a PE teacher and Deborah is bringing up her family. As for the others, Cameron wants to be a professional dancer but he can't get a break, they call him Michael Jackson number two, and Sally is a secretary for an American firm in Croydon.

It was pretty strange when I first came into this building to work, everybody seemed so distant. The people who came to the shop in those days treated me like a human being but they were much more conservative - what I call top-notch people. Right now people are more aggressive, maybe because the place is closing down and they are worried about their jobs.

The number of coloured people working here shot up about five years ago. I see quite a lot now, but that hasn't made any difference to what it is like for me working here. The customers are usually glad to see me and will ask for me if I am not about. Sometimes I have to remind them that I don't live at County Hall. Perhaps my popularity is due to how I present myself to people. Sometimes I feel really down, but as soon as I get through that door I change into "working me" and that is what people see. I feel that if I show my grumpiness they all will get grumpy too.

Our work is now controlled by a private firm so I don't know what I am going to do when the ILEA is abolished. I want a rest though; it has been non-stop for fourteen years. Apart from holidays, I've had just six days off. The company keeps asking me if I'll carry on working but I don't know - it depends on how tired I am. I'll miss the customers, but I want to go home, have a rest and spend some time on myself.

View from the Shop 2

William Israel talking to Sarah Olowe

William Israel went to Kennington Boys' School. He now lives with his partner in Stockwell. They have a four-year-old daughter.

I have worked in County Hall for about six years. I'm now a shop assistant. I replenish the shelves and do the cashiering when necessary. Originally I was downstairs in the cafeteria, mopping up round the back and making sure we had enough cutlery, plates and trays. After two years I was offered a chance to go upstairs, which I took in a flash because the cafeteria was getting a bit monotonous. There was no future in it, the money wasn't good, and obviously I wanted something better for myself.

Catering is not what I really wanted to do. I have three 'O' levels and used to work in a library but after a while I got bored of it and left. Then I found I could not get anything like it again. Now I am older I think I should have stuck at it. Even if I did not want to be a librarian I could have done something at the same level because I would have had the experience. I had the right qualifications to start as a clerical assistant but, though I got interview after interview, I could never get the jobs. Over a period of about six months I made countless applications from advertisements I found in the papers. When I started to get low on money, someone told me about getting work from a catering

company. That is how I came here. I had only been here for three
weeks when someone offered me a full-time job. My plan was to
find my feet and then get out. That was six years ago. It is a good
thing the ILEA is being abolished because it will force me to look
for other work.

In the shop I have met a lot of people other than the catering
staff, and I generally like it. The black politicians and officers of
the Authority often argue about the cost of things and generally
complain a lot. Some of them are rude and they often look
miserable. Maybe they have things on their minds, or maybe it is
pressure from work. I don't think they think I am one of them.

On the whole, County Hall is a friendly place but there are a lot
of people here who are not genuine. People will be friendly with
you as well as making it clear they think they are better than you.
Perhaps they think I've got nothing to say because I am wearing
overalls and they are dressed in a pinstripe suit. It is not choice
on my part. They give you a uniform and you have got to take care
of it. If I didn't wear it I'd be contravening the Hygiene Act. When
I'm at work I am a different person. In my own clothes I would
feel much freer and probably be a lot more confident as well. You
lack confidence because people treat you as if you haven't got any,
because of what you do. I suppose catering is the lowest form of
job you can have here anyway.

I went to Kennington Boys' School where the teachers came
across as quite encouraging. They obviously saw a bit of potential
in me, as with other boys, and they did their best to get it out of
us. I am a bit undecided about anti-racist education. To an
extent it is good because it gives black people and other ethnic
minorities a chance to do things that they might not have done
before. However, other people might think we are stirring up
trouble again, and there may be some people trying to promote
themselves and labelling it equal opportunities.

To my knowledge neither I nor any of the people I work with
have ever been asked our opinion about the Authority's equal
opportunities initiatives. I could understand there not being
enough time to come and talk to us but they might at least have
sent out a questionnaire.

A Personal Assistant

Sumitra Devi Tikaram

Sumitra Devi Tikaram has worked at County Hall for nine years. In the autumn of 1989 she became acting Personal Assistant to the Deputy Leader.

In 1981 I was offered an appointment as secretary/personal assistant to Tony Banks, the highly controversial Chairman of the Arts and Recreation Committee of the now defunct Greater London Council, who was a Labour Party Member for the constituency of Tooting. I was amazed when this happened as I consider myself to have been very naive politically and, in many ways, unaware of the problems faced by black people in London. For eighteen years I had lived a politically ignorant existence, not even bothering to cast a vote in any of the elections since my arrival in this country from the Pacific Islands of Fiji. I was dumbfounded to discover that I was a constituent of the man I had been appointed to work for! Usually, elected Members want the staff who work closely with them to be sympathetic to their political views. Mr Banks was decent enough to give me an opportunity to work with him despite my ignorance. If he had turned me down I imagine I would still be living in cuckoo land as far as my political awareness is concerned.

I felt very uncomfortable at first as I had been told that Mr Banks would prefer me to call him by his first name. Having worked for senior white officers in various local authorities in

London, I knew this was not the norm. It took me quite a while to get used to this as I could not easily forget my colonial upbringing, where all white people were considered superior to the locals and were discouraged from being on familiar terms with them.

Having come to terms with informal and easy-going relationships with all the elected Members of the majority party (that is, the Labour Members), I then had to get accustomed to the various revolutionary policies that were being implemented fast and furiously. The term "equal opportunities" became commonplace and every committee was required to ensure its implementation. By law the GLC/ILEA could not discriminate on the grounds of one's colour, race, sex, class, disability, religion or sexual orientation. This was hammered in at all levels of staffing and at the 1000 or so schools and colleges throughout inner London. The Ethnic Minorities Unit, the Disability Unit and the Women's Committee were all set up to monitor the anti-racist and anti-sexist policies. It was only then that I discovered the many disadvantages and the discrimination that existed with regard to women and the black population in London. Once the policies were implemented, not only did black people find themselves being given equal opportunities at almost all levels, but women came into their own and enjoyed such basic necessities as workplace crèches provided at County Hall for staff and for those attending meetings at various venues. Women were given grants for late-night door-to-door transport and for courses to encourage them to train for jobs that had been exclusively for men in the past. There was also help for the disabled and pensioners in the form of cheap transport, entertainment and general welfare requirements. These policies had a great impact on the lives of ordinary Londoners, especially the black women.

With the demise of the GLC, the new Inner London Education Authority came into existence in 1986 and I was fortunate enough to be transferred to work in the new setup. I am very aware that the ILEA has persevered with the policies introduced by its predecessor, indeed I have been one of the beneficiaries, but it took a long time for senior officers to understand that the Members were serious. People are much more aware now but, when these changes were first introduced staff who were set in their ways just could not stomach it.

Unfortunately, the ILEA's days are numbered, but I very much hope that the authorities who are empowered to run the education service after April 1990 will not hesitate to carry on the sterling work so courageously introduced and implemented by both the GLC and the ILEA.

Part II:
In the Community

School Governors

Out of Control

Paul Boateng MP talking to Sarah Olowe

Paul Boateng, MP for Brent South, was Chair of Governors at Priory Park School in south London from 1976 to 1981. Until 1987 he was Chair of the Afro-Caribbean Education Resource Project (ACER) which he co-founded with Len Garrison.

The ILEA has done some wonderful things and I do not believe there is really any other way to organise inner London education other than through a body like the ILEA. I deeply regret its abolition, but I think it would be a great mistake if, in the course of lamenting its passing, we were to pretend that all had been rosy, because it was not.

In comparison to other educational authorities, the ILEA has not made massive inroads into the deep-rooted disadvantage under which black pupils suffer. On the contrary, the rhetoric has often hidden some very bad practices and some very real neglect of educational need.

My experience was of an educational authority and a bureaucracy that was often very far removed from what was going on on the ground. It was very hard to get that bureaucracy to deliver to the schools. I am not only talking about equal opportunities, I am talking about things like getting gas cupboards for the science lab, and about general repairs. The bureaucracy was very often intransigent and pig-headed. The idea that it was all a haven of best practice, sensitivity and service delivery is an absolute nonsense.

The servicing of committees and of the governors by the local education office for the district was, in the main, quite good and one had a good relationship with the local divisional office. The problems came in the relations with County Hall. I felt that senior officers of the ILEA were not sufficiently controlled by Members. Some of them did exactly as they pleased; one in particular did exactly as he wanted for years and Members seemed quite unable to stop him. Officers would fail to provide the information necessary for Members to make a decision, Members were misled, and there was slowness in carrying out decisions. When Members became involved in disputes, if they took any side other than that of the officers, they seemed to get into hot water very quickly as the officers would run campaigns against them.

As a result of the input of black Members the Authority certainly became much more aware of the needs and aspirations of black parents. However, I am not sure that black Members were actually able to affect the system that much because for a long time the bureaucracy stymied and frustrated them.

The story of the ILEA would have been very different had it been led by someone like Herman Ouseley six years ago. It wasn't, and it is a great tragedy for the ILEA that it took abolition for Herman Ouseley to be appointed as Chief Executive. He is a first-class administrator, has a deep understanding of the way institutions work and a deep understanding of the needs and concerns of the black community. I think he would have got the bureaucracy by the short and curlies and forced it to deliver.

Education shapes our whole life opportunity and, all too often, it has distorted the life opportunities of black children. I was a governor from about 1975 to 1981. What I wanted to do was to be part and parcel of trying to get the ILEA's system to become more responsive and sensitive to the views of parents and to the needs of black and white working-class children. I think the main power one has as a governor is in relation to teacher appointments and attempts to influence the ethos of the school in that way. This is very important and not to be underestimated.

The life chances and expectations of black and white working-class children have decreased over the past ten years. It is very depressing. In the mid-to-late seventies there was an idealistic group of young black teachers who began to come into the system;

of these the vast majority have now left. That is a terrible indictment because these are the very young black men and women who were educated, managed to survive, and got through. When they came back into the system they found it had no place for them. And whilst all that was going on there was all this talk and rhetoric about equal opportunities.

I believe there was an addiction on the part of some politicians to the rhetoric of equal opportunities without any real engagement of their hearts and minds in the issues of performance and delivery. Excellence, fullstop, has been a dirty word in some quarters of the ILEA. People who come from backgrounds where excellence is taken for granted appear to undervalue it, either out of guilt, misplaced ideology, or indifference, or indeed an underestimation of what working-class children have to offer. It may also be due to laziness; it is hard work stimulating children.

The ILEA failed to provide a context in which low expectations on the part of teachers were consistently challenged. However, in other situations I have seen teachers coming from a position of ignorance or indeed hostility who have genuinely learnt and have done some marvellous work. At ACER, I saw how it was possible to change teachers' thinking and attitudes, not by grand statements, but by actually getting people in a group situation and working through the issues.Then it is possible to build and develop materials together and get away from the 'send me the multi-racial pack' idea, which is a trap teachers can very often fall into because they are under so much pressure. At ACER, teachers addressed the issue of how to counter prejudice and racism, how to utilise existing materials and create new ones. They actually came to recognise that genuine multi-racial education and education for a multi-racial society applies to all schools, regardless of how many black children there are in them.

Two Generations

Mary Jeremiah-Baldry talking to Sarah Olowe

Mary Jeremiah Baldry went to ILEA primary and secondary schools. She trained as a musician and is now a theatre administrator. She is Chair of Governors at her children's school, Ennersdale Junior and Infants, in Lewisham, south London.

I remember being told at school about the necessity of washing your hands. I was five or six. I said, 'I don't have to wash a lot because I'm brown', probably to get out of it. The teacher asked my mother whether I honestly believed this. When my own daughter was five she was hand-printing after school. The black children did brown hand-prints and the white children did pink hand-prints. My daughter was given pink paint. I am quite light-skinned; my daughter is lighter-skinned than me. No doubt she will be politically black when she is older, but we are not dealing with that yet. When I complained the teachers insisted she was white. They explained by saying that when you buy cosmetics you rub them on your wrist and you find the right tone for your face...It was humiliating to have to educate people who consider themselves well-educated and professional. Recently I was asked to read one of the Anancy, or spider, stories because I could read it with the right accent. I kept a straight face and read in the accent I use all the time – south London. Teachers have been through ILEA schools, gone to teacher-training college, and then gone back into ILEA schools and yet they don't know anything.

When you are black and everyone else is white you stick out like mad. One school I went to was massive, over 2000 pupils. But there were hardly any black children and none in my year. I was twelve and I was big and I was loud and I was good. That does not go down well when the people around you are small, very white and fairly quiet.

My best subject was music. I went to the Centre for Young Musicians, the ILEA's Saturday school, and played in the concert band every holiday. There weren't many black children at CYM or in the London Schools' Symphony Orchestra. If you lived in Barnes you were probably a white person and your school would have a good orchestra. If you lived in Wandsworth you would probably have a steel band.

My reports, even the music ones, were quite racist, remarking on my 'natural rhythm and ability'. There is nothing natural about my ability; it cost thousands of pounds to train me as a musician. I wasn't born "naturally" able to use a word processor, but I can use one really efficiently now.

There were some really good teachers, ones without an ounce of fundamental racism in them. They were like little rays of sun, but most of the time at school I felt inadequate. Without my parents' support I would not be where I am now because nobody else expected me to do well. My father was from Trinidad and my mother was born here. They found it difficult dealing with ILEA schools even though they were teachers themselves.

I took my English 'O' level when I was fourteen instead of sixteen. I told my mother I thought I could do it – other kids were doing it early. My mother went to the parents' evening to be told that I would 'definitely fail'; she disagreed and offered to pay. I got a grade B. It was weird having positive forces at home and such large negative forces at school. I honestly feel some teachers were fearful of what I could achieve.

I became Chair of Governors because my children were underachieving. I didn't like the local fee-paying schools and I didn't want to send the children to boarding schools where I'd have even less say in what happened to them. The governors' responsibilities are mainly pastoral. We interview heads and deputy heads, but headteachers interview teaching staff. We make sure that equal opportunity policies are administered and that children aren't excluded from school trips because they can't afford it. If something isn't up to scratch we talk to the head who will then see the person responsible for that area. Then we will visit.

Out of twelve governors, four are black. I feel we have raised the status of black parents within the school. We've squashed all the fallacies – that black people can't turn up on time, can't do this, can't do that, can't write, can't make telephone calls, have no discipline and so on. This is what schools were saying to us and what they've always said. Schools have got to accept black children as English children with English parents.

One governor set up a meeting for parents. They wanted bullying to be stamped out, better school meals, uniforms, cleaner toilets, and to know what their children were doing and what they were expected to learn each week. They also wanted to know what they should be doing to help – reading, projects and so on. The teachers didn't read the letter properly and closed ranks, assuming it was critical. In fact they were doing a lot of these things already.

I don't like being Chair. I was beaten up by another governor who didn't see that people like me must have a big say in what happens in the school. I shouldn't have to take on this burden, but I will go on so that my children and their contemporaries have the chance to do well.

You are lucky if you are born in London as opposed to say Bradford or the Isle of Wight. At least here the equal opportunities policies have been laid down. I was thirty before I was able to call someone a racist. I can do it now. It is not for me to excuse them. If I feel a teacher holds an attitude that is not good for my children, that teacher will not teach my children. It was easy for teachers to tell my parents that I was not good enough, particularly my father as he was an immigrant. As a parent I will be more demanding. Nobody will tell me that my children are not good enough. I am not an immigrant. I belong here and my children belong here. The colour of their skin should be immaterial to their achievement. It won't be easy, but I refuse to opt out.

Teachers

Controlling Black Children

Lincoln Williams

Lincoln Williams taught at Ernest Bevin School from the mid seventies until the early eighties when he became Head of the Youth Centre attached to the school. He worked for the Youth Service for several years and is now Southwark's Community Education Officer. Mr Williams went to ILEA schools but left without any qualifications. He gained his basic education by taking evening classes at Southwark College.

I can remember vividly the interview at which I was appointed. It was clear that the panel had not interviewed many black people before. The Chair went out of his way to make jokey and flippant remarks about race. I assume such comments were attempts to reduce the tension of what was a difficult situation for them. As a student, fresh from university and teacher training college, I did not feel strong enough to challenge such statements; after all I needed the job badly. It was my first interview and I felt I did well.

In those days interview panels made their decisions on the spot and all the candidates waited. The clerk to the governors came out and asked me to go back in. I knew then, as did the other candidates, that they had decided to appoint me. When I went in the first thing the Chair said to me was, 'You would have sued us if we had not appointed you, wouldn't you?' It was not until much later that I realised the personal and institutional racism involved in that appointment. That uneasy and slightly sullied feeling has remained with me and always will. That was my introduction to the ILEA.

The circumstances of my appointment, however, were just hors d'oeuvres compared to what was in store for me once in the post. The school had recently merged with a boys' grammar to form a large comprehensive, and many of the former grammar school teachers resented this very much. That the school now employed black teachers confirmed their worst fears. Many of them could not bring themselves to talk to me, and some of them left the school without even acknowledging my existence. This was in 1976, in a school where forty percent of the pupils were black. In addition, I soon learnt that at least two teachers had explicitly racist attitudes and were not afraid to let the black pupils know about them. It was clear, however, that no one in a senior management position was prepared to take action against them. How many black pupils' school careers were either terminated through suspension or made difficult by teachers like these? Their school records will only show the cause of their suspension as perceived by the teacher. There was no legitimate form of resistance open to such pupils. Thus they could resist in the only way left to them, and that way ensured their failure in the education system.

The late seventies saw the rise of the multi-cultural education movement. My school resisted this movement for as long as it could. It took a vicious playground incident and the National Front selling literature outside the school before a small group of teachers got the go-ahead to draw up a policy statement and guidelines for handling racial incidents. The policy statement went out to all parents of first year pupils – I cannot remember the guidelines ever being used.

The multi-cultural education movement also increased the pressure to employ more black teachers. It was a tremendous relief to me when several other black teachers were appointed. This gave us strength even if it was just at the level of seeing each other and sharing our experiences. Our presence reduced the number of racist comments in the staff room but it also began to fuel the inevitable white backlash.

When I was appointed deputy head of the fourth year it was because the school had identified a sizeable group of "bad" black boys and thought I should be able to handle them. If I could not, then it would only go to prove that they were uncontrollable – a vindication of the traditional stereotype of young black people. If I succeeded then the solution to such problems would be to employ more black teachers who understood the culture of the black pupils and would make excellent role models for them. Then the pupils would learn to try and make it in the system, rather than oppose it. Teachers like myself would be on show, especially in assemblies, as a symbol for black pupils. It was hoped that the "code" embodied in me on the stage would be decoded by the pupils to read: maybe as a race we cannot succeed, but if I work hard enough and am a "good nigger" they may allow me the privilege of becoming a teacher, or a social worker, or a youth worker, because they know that I can control young black people better than they can.

In such situations black teachers, black youth workers and other black workers in the caring professions find themselves having to be a lot stricter than their white colleagues, because the cost of failure is too great. Should they fail, it would reinforce negative stereotypes of black people's abilities. As black social controllers we know that we are fighting a battle we cannot win.

I have now left, but often visit the school. Personal and institutional racism are still at work. Some things have changed, however; black youngsters now constitute the majority of pupils, and the school has a black headteacher and a black deputy. Such appointments may be the only tangible success to have come out of the ILEA's anti-racist/equal opportunities policies.

It must be remembered that anti-racist policies were not adopted as something desired by the white administration at County Hall. They were fought for by black parents and teachers, who saw and opposed the damage a racist education system was doing to black pupils. For them it was clear that the ILEA was failing their children, and that a large factor in this failure was the inherent racism of the structure coupled with the personal racism of a sizeable number of teachers. If the Authority wanted to counter the rise in the movement for supplementary schools, and counter the calls from black parents for separate schools, then they had to undertake some initiatives. Multi-cultural education, then, was a strategy to try and retain the faith of black parents in the education system.

In the early eighties I went into the Youth Service and found that no thought was being given to equal opportunities and anti-racist policies. Many of us fought for their adoption by the Youth Service, but we lost. I have outlined elsewhere the reasons for our failure.[1] Here it is enough to say that personal and institutional racism are still rife in the Youth Service and that policies have had very little effect on practice. Many more black workers and officers are being employed in the Service, but this is due to our perceived role as better social controllers of potential rioters rather than the operation of any equal opportunity policy.

1. Williams, L O, *Partial Surrender – Race and Resistance in the Youth Service,* London, The Falmer Press, 1988.

Improving the Arrangement

Saleh Mamon

Saleh Mamon is the Secretary of the Inner London Black Teachers' Group and General Inspector (Science) for Islington's Education Service. He was born in Nairobi and has taught in both Kenya and Great Britain. Mr Mamon worked as an ILEA teacher for eighteen years. He specialises in zoology.

The drop in the number of children in London in the eighties led to the re-organisation of ILEA schools and the redeployment of teachers. Surplus teachers have been labelled in many ways; they were initially called supernumary teachers, but the latest fashion is to call them "teachers above authorised numbers" (TAANs).

Black teachers were hit badly by all the redeployment exercises. In the early days the ILEA did not monitor the process for equal opportunities so schools were able to shed their black teachers, even though many of them were working in shortage subject areas. By 1984 a clear pattern had emerged and the Inner London Black Teachers' Group (ILBTG) launched a campaign against the racial discrimination that was discreetly taking place. The ILEA responded by setting up a working party on the "Criteria of Redeployment of Teachers" which was chaired by Gerry Davis. The working party invited black teachers' groups to make submissions and its report recommended a revision of the existing criteria and the monitoring of the entire redeployment process. It stressed that equal opportunities considerations should be an integral part of schools' decisions about curriculum needs. Three years after the report was written the ILBTG discovered that, although the ILEA's officers had selected some of its ideas, the document had never gone to the Education Committee and, therefore, its recommendations did not have a chance of becoming ILEA policy.

One consequence of redeployment was that many black teachers in mainstream subjects were encouraged to take up supply teaching which is on a higher pay scale. The teachers themselves accepted these posts because there was not the remotest chance of them getting promotion where they were. However, by doing this, the Authority unwittingly created a supply pool largely made up of black teachers.

After the detailed monitoring of redeployment began in 1986, sixty percent of the black teachers identified for redeployment were found to be located in nine schools. The investigation which ensued became known as "The Nine Schools Review" and was carried out by two black inspectors, Mike Hussey and Bruce Gill. Their report said, 'The devastatingly negative effect of the exercise upon black teachers must not be under-estimated. The Authority is confronted with a major task of repair and support which will extend well into the future.' They recommended that several black teachers should be reinstated, and asked the Authority to implement the recommendations of the Davis Report and formulate an explicit policy with regard to the career and professional development of black teachers.

During this period the ILEA had taken and implemented a decision to reorganise the schools in Wandsworth which involved merging ten schools into five. We had reports that black teachers were losing out in the process, and when figures finally became available this was the picture:

The Number of Black Teachers

	Before	After	Change
Scale 4	3	3	0
Scale 3	8	3	−5
Scale 2	6	5	−1
Scale 1	13	19	+6
TOTAL	30	30	

The proportion of black teachers holding posts of responsibility had dropped significantly and more were found at the bottom of the career ladder.

During the 1987-88 redeployment exercise evidence emerged of the misuse of Section 11 funding and discrimination of a similar pattern to that in Wandsworth. In April 1988 the ILBTG raised the matter formally and informally with the ILEA's officers and Members. It was found that in some schools (which served a large black community) between a third to a half of the black teachers had been identified for redeployment. A statistical trawl revealed twenty schools that had identified black teachers disproportionately.

The ILBTG demanded an enquiry into these schools and the ILEA set up a team of two – Mike Hussey from the Multi-Ethnic Inspectorate and Simon Bird from the Personnel Branch – to conduct detailed investigations in four of the twenty schools. The report was ready in January 1989 and was submitted to the Chief Inspector. A summary of the report was also prepared. In March 1989 the Chief Inspector presented her report to the Education Officer. We were told in writing by officers and Members that the reports would soon be made public, but by July it had become clear that a policy decision had been taken to suppress the reports. It wasn't until September 1989 that the Education Officer, David Mallen, presented his report to the Equal Opportunity Sub-Committee. This report said that no racial discrimination had occurred, attributing the over-identification of black teachers to their small numbers and lower positions in schools. It is difficult to believe that a senior officer of an authority that is an equal opportunity employer can have made such a statement! How can he have overlooked the whole point of having an equal opportunities policy? Fortunately the earlier reports were leaked to the press and it became obvious why the ILEA officers and Members colluded to suppress them.

The original report found that black teachers were twice as likely to be identified and moved during redeployment as white teachers. It confirmed that the teacher redeployment exercise had had a devastating effect on black teachers' careers. Eighty-eight percent of the black teachers interviewed reported that their position had declined quite significantly; some were in despair due to their redeployment. In the case of one of the four schools, the report found clear evidence of discrimination and misuse of Section 11 funding. With respect to Section 11 funding the investigators reported that the school had 'redistributed resources from named postholders to teachers who are not themselves named postholders. Actions of this kind require Home Office approval.' They discovered that seven teachers with bilingual skills were identified for movement when the school had four full-time vacancies in this area. The school had also failed to submit Section 11 returns in accordance with Home Office requirements.

Marshalling all the evidence and considering mitigating circumstances, the report concluded that:

> None of this, however, can fully explain the contradictions that appear to emerge from the decisions taken regarding TAANS (surplus teachers). The discrepancies that surround decisions cover every major area; the curriculum, Section 11, validity of volunteers and general deployment of teachers. The most alarming aspect of all this has been the effect on the black teachers and in turn its repercussions on the black and ethnic minority pupils.

Although the investigators did not find it possible to say whether the headteachers had intended to be discriminatory, they found from their evidence that the headteachers' decisions had produced a discriminatory effect. Even worse, the enquiry implicated one of the ILEA's Assistant Education Officers by inferring from the evidence that:

> The position taken by the then Assistant Education Officer/SEC is one of a very serious nature because he does not appear to have addressed the concerns that were referred to him by the Chairs of the Appeals panel. In doing so he appears to be a party to actions that have been implemented with the effect of discriminating against black teachers.

Of the eight recommendations made by the report, the following two called for firm action by the ILEA:

1) Any employee involved in endorsing or instigating actions leading to discriminatory effects should be subject to investigations under the Discipline section of the Staff Code.

2) Further consideration should be given to the possibility of financial compensation as an appropriate form of redress for all black teachers covered by the enquiry where it has been proved that they have suffered damage to their career prospects as a direct consequence of discrimination.

The suppression of the above report and its recommendations sets the final seal on the ILEA's record in equal opportunities. Only an open, independent enquiry will bring the full truth out into the public domain. Social justice demands that the ILEA, before its timely demise, should reinstate to the post they held before the redeployment exercise of 1987-88 every black teacher who was a victim of racial discrimination and is still in service. Those who were forced out of teaching should be given adequate redress for the loss of their career.

The attempt at a cover-up is particularly deplorable when the ILEA has publicly launched a new deal for black teachers under its "positive action of equality" initiative and is recruiting black teachers from the Caribbean and Bangladesh. The black community now knows that these are meaningless gestures when the ILEA is failing to retain the black teachers it has, and failing to act against those who have clearly discriminated both directly and indirectly on grounds of race.

It is quite clear that bureaucratic equal opportunity policies have failed to change the position of black people in British society. Such policies are a reaction to the upsurge of discontent in the black community and in some ways are designed to contain it. The only guarantee of winning social and political equality in post-imperialist Britain and the newly emerging Europe is through the struggle and self-organisation of the black and ethnic minority communities themselves. Our slogan for the future should not just be equal opportunities; it should be empowerment. Power to the people.

How Redeployment Affected Me

Robert Ridyard talking to Sarah Olowe

In 1987 Robert Ridyard was selected for compulsory transfer from Blackheath Blue Coat School where he had taught for seven years. In 1989 he was appointed catering lecturer at South East London College. Although not all Mr Ridyard's work involves children with special needs, he is especially committed to working with them.

When you look at the murky business that goes on in the ILEA despite its equal opportunities policies, it is easy to see why so little has changed over the years. The system is only as good as the people it appoints and the autonomy afforded to school inspectors and headteachers means that it is almost impossible to remove them when things go wrong.

I was one of those teachers who, marked for transfer from their school, found they had nowhere else to go. I had many very supportive friends and colleagues who valued my work; but were it not for the stubborn intervention of a senior politician, who forced South East London College to take me, I would certainly be out of education.

During my teaching career I unwittingly gained the misnomer of "black radical" within the Department of Education. I was sacked by Surrey County Council for challenging "authority", and subsequently accepted temporary contracts at South East London College (SELTEC) and at Blackheath Blue Coat School. I discovered a rapport existed between myself and Blue Coat School's behaviourally disturbed children. After six months,

Sheila Houliston, the headteacher at the time, offered me a permanent contract. I found myself working for an apparently enlightened education authority with a supportive headteacher who encouraged you to speak your mind. What followed were three of my happiest and most productive years in education.

I taught catering and, though my children may not have been academics, they were nevertheless very talented. The school was written about in the press because we took catering seriously. We prepared many lunches, dinners, buffets and prize-givings and we tried to develop the students' confidence further by taking them on trips to central London and abroad. Providing a high-level course was not cheap. Many of the children came from the surrounding areas of Deptford and Lewisham rather than prosperous Blackheath, but no child was prevented from taking part because they couldn't afford it.

In 1983 Sheila Houliston retired. Our new headteacher was not a great success. I tried to challenge his racism but found much of it was directed at me. When I explained that things would be much easier if he showed some goodwill he replied, 'I am not running a democracy.' I was later told that the catering and the home economics departments could be merged, which would stop me attending heads of department meetings, and that if I didn't like it I could leave.

Over the years many teachers did leave the school and so did many black children who were expelled. By 1986 we had lost our entire senior management team, the chairman of the governors, two heads of house, the head of English, the head of modern languages, the head of special needs, the teachers in charge of drama, home economics, textiles and child development, plus the school secretary, the school librarian and the assistant librarian. I wrote about my concerns in the quinquennial review, a five year assessment which heads of department complete for the inspectorate. My comments were fair criticisms under the circumstances but the headteacher and the home economics and catering inspector were infuriated. Shortly after this I was earmarked for transfer. I was advised that I had a sound appeal case because so many of the procedures adopted were incorrect. The panel was sympathetic but my appeal was turned down. I refused an offer of redundancy with a pension because I wanted to carry on working.

A black colleague who had accompanied me to the appeal board put my case to the Deputy Leader, Anstey Rice. I then met Anstey and other Members who helped by repeatedly instructing officers to deal with my case. However, the officers concerned rarely responded and for a long time nothing was done.

I decided that if I was going to be transferred I wanted to go somewhere that was alright. I had some misgivings about SELTEC, but because I had worked there before I had many friends and acquaintances who I knew would be supportive. I was told that there were no vacancies in the Hotel and Catering Studies Department at SELTEC. At the eleventh hour I discovered that this information was false. I contacted the Authority to tell them of the situation and in the event no external appointment was made.

Eventually I was called to SELTEC for what I believed would be a placement discussion. It turned out to be a full-blown interview with seven interviewers (a placement discussion should have two). The interview was a fiasco; it was obvious that I was not wanted and the process adopted was clearly designed to rubbish and humiliate me. Apart from me, the only other black person at the interview was the multi-ethnic representative. However, unlike the white interviewers present, he was not taken out of the room for a private discussion prior to the interview. I was told later that the interviewers wanted the multi-ethnic representative to support the majority in order to make my rejection unanimous. The attitude was, 'This man is trouble, we don't want him.' The multi-ethnic inspector refused their request. I had good references from my former heads of department at SELTEC and Blackheath Blue Coat School and another reference from a rebel inspector, but these didn't help. SELTEC rejected me verbally.

I told the Members about the SELTEC interview in December 1988. The interview and the events surrounding my transfer made them painfully aware of how difficult it was for their policies to be implemented. Four months after SELTEC's informal decision I had another interview with them at which the head of the ILEA's redeployment unit, my NUT representative and two members of SELTEC staff were present. Shortly afterwards I was formally offered the post of catering lecturer.

I am not a radical, but like any good teacher I care deeply about the people I teach. I believe that the establishment is ruthless in its attempts to marginalise black people and what we say. In my case I was fortunate to find someone with the power to force an institution to change its mind. Others are not so lucky and a person with less tenacity would have gone to the wall.

A Coloured Lady on the Staff

Hyacinth Meerabux

Hyacinth Meerabux is currently Director of the Afro-Caribbean Education Resource Project. Before joining the ACER she worked as a classroom teacher in both London and Guyana.

'Why don't you visit the divisional office?', my friend said to me after I had been living in London for about three months and was beginning to show signs of boredom. She had settled here three years earlier and worked as a teacher. She gave me a telephone number and an address.

My meeting with the Divisional Inspector of the ILEA turned out to be a mini-interview, raising questions about basic qualifications, initial teacher training and teaching experience. After eligibility to teach in the division had been established, I was advised to provide verification of certificates and training so that the Department of Education and Science could assess my qualifications and issue me with a number.

I was born, educated and trained as a teacher in Guyana under the British colonials system. That training equipped me to teach just as efficiently in England as in Guyana. When I was offered the position of supply teacher, I was thrilled. I thought: 'Good, now I will be able to translate into practice all those theories that I could not adequately implement in Guyana because of the lack of resources.'

I shall always remember the 27th November 1958. It was a cold, foggy day and I was to report to a school to replace a teacher who was unwell. I arrived there and explained to the secretary that I was a teacher sent by the divisional office. 'Sit in there,' she ordered, pointing towards an anteroom, 'and wait for the headteacher's instructions.' Some time elapsed before she emerged from the head's room and asked me to follow her to the classroom.

The secretary did not ask my name. She just told the group of about twenty-five second-year junior children that I would be their teacher for the rest of the afternoon. As soon as she left the questioning began. What was my name? Which country was I from? Was I a real teacher? And then the remark, 'We've never had a coloured teacher before'. In those days "coloured" was the word used to describe black people.

At the end of the day, I returned to the anteroom to get the attendance form signed. It was the secretary who once again spoke to me. She apologised for her behaviour earlier and added that she had never seen a "coloured" teacher before! Furthermore, she thought I was after a cleaning job. I need not describe the expression on my face. I was livid. I had never been "mistaken" for a cleaner in Guyana. When the form was returned to me, I left the building without the courtesy of an introduction to the head. That evening I reflected upon the events of the day and I said to myself, 'Not a very good start to teaching in London, not a very good start at all.'

Happily, my first day as a supply teacher was not an indicator of days to come. I worked in several schools on short and long-term bases. There were days when it took skill and courage to engage the children in gainful work, while on other occasions it was relatively easy to motivate them.

I had little social contact with teachers at the staffroom level. I have never been able to establish whether this was because of my blackness or if it was their normal attitude to new teachers. However, I was determined to continue.

My application for a permanent post was successful and in January 1960 I was sent to a school in a road called Paradise. Nothing was further from paradise than that school. The building was old and set in depressing surroundings. One morning there was a small group of mothers standing by the gate, chatting. As I walked by there was silence and then I heard 'Mind the blackbird', followed by subdued laughter. I walked on. I mentioned it to the head and he laughed and muttered something about ignoring the retched people. I felt deeply offended and said so.

Another memorable incident concerned a child who was an habitual late comer, although she lived about two streets away. When asked why she was always late, the child replied that she had to wait for her mum to wake up and bring her to school. I said to the child, 'Ask mummy to try and get you here earlier.' The next morning the mother walked into the classroom and said, 'I don't take advice from teachers, let alone black ones.' With those words, she stormed out of the room. I reported the incident to the head, who said that he would deal with it. I received no apology from the parent, the head did not raise the matter with me again. However, the child was removed from my class and put in a parallel one. It seemed incredible that a head would deal with staffing concerns in such an insensitive way. I was not unhappy to leave the school.

My next appointment came in 1961. It was to a school in a similar area, run by a head who, I later found out, had a heart of gold. Our introduction was brief. 'Tell me a little about yourself and the schools you've worked in,' he said. When I had finished he informed me that there was already a "coloured" lady on the staff and that there were no problems. 'Let me say this to you,' he continued, 'if you don't like it you go. If I don't like it you go.' 'How brutal', I thought, but I remained there for eight and a half years.

It was a mixed junior school, and although I taught the third years for some time, my expressed preference was for the first years. It was with first year children that I was able to put my ideas into practice.

I regarded the first term at school as the "bread and butter" term because it was during that time that I endeavoured to find out the children's strengths and weaknesses in order to teach, reinforce and extend. This was particularly so in relation to reading, writing and mathematics. Organising the group needed skill, ingenuity and patience. I found that when the children understood the purpose of an exercise they were able to work on their own, help each other, or seek help from the class or school library. In this way I gained time to devote attention to children who were less motivated and needed individual help. Eventually, children were able to distinguish between activities given to them to keep them quite and those regarded as important. Discipline was rarely a problem because the children understood my limits. Nevertheless, when potential troublemakers attempted to disrupt the work of the class, the head's backing was always forthcoming. When a mother objected to 'that black teacher' making her son do needlework, the head saw the situation as a parent attempting to undermine his teacher's authority and firmly told her that she could take her child elsewhere if she didn't like what I was doing. The boy remained in my class.

I've changed my mind about things I've done with the children, and I've questioned myself on many occasions about whether I was doing the right thing by them. My conclusion is that I've failed in some areas and succeeded in others.

There were no black children in my classes and the fact that I was black did not seem to matter to the children. One parent came to the classroom seeking permission for her son to leave early. When she saw me she said, 'But John didn't tell me his teacher was...' 'Black,' I added, and smiled. This seemed to make her feel less uncomfortable.

During the 1960's the word "racism" was never mentioned in my presence in any staffroom conversation. However, words and phrases like "hyper", "aggressive", "violent", "can't cope with freedom" and "jungle life" were all used frequently in relations to the behaviour of the few black children just entering the schools. Teacher relationships remained friendly enough in most cases, but one incident has always remained with me. When a senior post was offered to an Asian teacher, an elderly white teacher thought that the post should have been given to a white colleague. She said to me one morning, 'Did you hear that Mrs Z has now become the senior female teacher?' I replied that I had heard. She continued, 'I'm surprised; after all Mrs Z is not one of us.' My reply was, 'Nor am I.' There was a pregnant pause after which she left the staffroom. I was shocked and particularly dismayed because I knew Mrs Z and the elderly teacher were very friendly and visited each other's homes.

I had many satisfying moments teaching in London schools and when I returned to Guyana in 1970 I took with me an experience which was gratifying. I also firmly believe that my blackness was not as important a factor as my ability to function as an effective teacher.

After an absence of ten years, I returned to London, once again as a supply teacher. I noticed that changes had taken place in the children's behaviour; there were many playground fights as a result of name-calling and racial slurs. Significant, too, was the fact that racism as an issue was being openly discussed in staffrooms. Not all teachers took part in the discussions though, and unfortunatley it was the converted who attended racism awareness courses and tried to translate the theory into practice.

I subsequently learned that many of these changes were the result of the ILEA's multi-ethnic initiatives, as well as pressure from community groups and black organisations such as the Afro-Caribbean Education Resource Project (ACER), where I am currently employed.

ACER was set up as a partnership between the Afro-Caribbean community and the ILEA. Its main brief is to repond to the needs ot the Afro-Caribbean community by developing high-quality, innovative learning materials that are both educationally relevant and culturally diverse. We are also responsible for designing the "I'm Special" materials which have been widely acclaimed by teachers, social workers and parents. ACER also conduct seminars and workshops to help teachers make the best use of our materials and develop school policies. All our work in schools has been facilitated by the ILEA and the team is accountable to the Authority professionally through the Multi-Ethnic Inspectorate.

There is still much to be done in schools to achieve equality of experience and equality of opportunity. The ILEA issued a challenge. As I write, the disbanding of the Authority and the transfer of education to the boroughs is taking place. I sincerely hope that the London boroughs individually will carry forward the work so boldly started by the ILEA.

Steel Pans

Gerald Forsyth talking to Sarah Olowe

Gerry Forsyth is responsible for bringing steel pans to the ILEA. He has worked for the Authority since 1969 and is currently the ILEA's Steel Pans Organiser.

I had been teaching the pans privately to an English teacher called John Rutherford, who worked at Paddington Lower School, when I was approached by his headteacher and asked to teach the children as well. Things developed from there and by 1978 there were about fifty schools with steel pans. The steel band world was still very small in England, so I knew all the good people. I was subsequently appointed Steel Pans Advisor and worked closely with the Music Inspector, Audrey Dennett, until she retired three years ago.

In the old days, the Authority had problems employing steel band tutors and buying instruments. The trade was making a good profit selling the ILEA all their worn-out instruments; they argued that the Authority couldn't tell the difference.

Steel band is underrated both inside and outside English education, but, nevertheless, not everyone can be taught to play. Also, youngsters are often sent to me for the wrong reasons. It took me a long time to realise that I was being sent children who the school considered a problem. Many of them were well behaved, probably because they enjoyed what they were doing. The pans can be used as a form of therapy, but only if the children enjoy it. I've had some remarkable children. One boy was sent to me because he was always getting into fights. He found it was much more satisfying to beat his frustration into the drums. That same boy later became a very fine steel pans teacher. However, it is unrealistic to send a child who can't learn anything. You have to be fairly intelligent to learn music from memory.

The children in ILEA schools have one three-quarter hour group lesson a week. That divides into five minutes per child. We make good progress, but it isn't easy. The Inner London School Steel Orchestra (LSSO) is supposed to contain the city's best young musicians, but there are very good young players in London who are unable to travel all the way to the Centre for Young Musicians, in Victoria, for special lessons, so the LSSO really consists of the children who are interested and who can come.

When I visit schools I always advise teachers not to let the band play out too soon. Just like any other instrument, with the pans you have to do a lot of repetitive work in order to acquire the necessary dexterity. Some people teach tunes parrot-fashion, that is, without doing any basic music. That sort of approach is alright if you only want to learn one or two tunes (some audiences are content to hear "Yellow Bird" all the time), but it's not much good for anything else.

If a headteacher wants to start a steel band in his/her school, I always ask why, and they often reply by muttering something about the children's culture. I think most teachers encourage steel pans because they want to give black children something they and their parents will appreciate and I think this attitude is wrong. The steel pan is a musical instrument and must be played by everybody; you don't say, 'only the white children can play the piano.' More black children play the pans than white children, but some of my best players are Asian children, and steel pans are certainly not part of their parents' culture.

There is a lot of snobbery in the music world and many people think paper qualifications are everything. You don't need to go to the Guildhall or the London School of Music to learn pans but I have been approached by people who cannot distinguish between having a good musical training and special knowledge of a particular instrument. A lady from Trinidad was sent here once to fetch some adjudicators for a steel band festival. They could have found people in the Caribbean, of course, but everybody knows somebody's cousin there, and they wanted people they could trust to be unbiased. The lady asked me to go, and said she also wanted somebody from the Guildhall School of Music. I just laughed. You need to have heard the pans before you can judge which one is better than the next. Steel band music has a complex rhythmical structure which is not well understood by most European musicians. An English woman like Audrey Dennett, who has been around the pans for years, would know, and English children who have grown up with the sound of the pans will know which band sounds better; but a guy who has never listened – how can he understand? He would listen to a noise and not know what he was listening for.

I don't want to say too much about it, but the amount of racism present in the schools I visit disappoints me. Our work involves travelling from school to school, but nowadays I send white staff to do basic work on the pans because of the racism directed at black workers. We are often treated like a security risk whereas the white workers I send are rarely challenged about their right to be on the school premises.

It's a fact of life that music teachers often consider whether they are giving the children something useful, or whether it would be better to encourage them in subjects that would give them a higher chance of earning a living. There is some work tuning the instruments and I know about a dozen people who are living well just by playing pans. There is room for more, and it is certainly better than working in dead-end jobs.

Constantly Undermined

Sybil Naidu

Sybil Naidu is currently an Equal Opportunities Advisory Teacher for Ealing Education Service. She trained as a teacher in England and South Africa.

My final ILEA appointment as an advisory teacher to inner London's secondary schools left me surprised and bemused. For seven years I had taught in the Authority with little prospect of being promoted and on my many trips across London visiting schools I had the time to reflect on how this had come about.

I was first appointed as an English teacher at a south London comprehensive. I had worked in industry before going into teaching and during my probationary year I found myself in charge of a pilot English and business communication course which involved supervising two teachers. Like many colleagues I took on responsibilities within the department and across the school. As I believe the pleasure of reading is worth promotion among pupils I ran the school workshop, without renumeration, but discovered that running a pet club and looking after lost property were considered even worthier, as those jobs were scaled posts.

I introduced the teaching of African and Caribbean literature to the English department and included it in the 'A' level course. A short while later, in collaboration with a few concerned colleagues, I organised a staff anti-racism conference and developed the school's policy on race. Consequently, when I applied for a scaled post in the department, the inspector, at my interview, recommended that I pursue a career as an advisory teacher for multi-cultural education. However, he did not offer me the job I was applying for.

Although I made several applications over the years, I was only ever given acting scale posts. I had at least three major areas of responsibility. At this time there was the dubious practice of advertising posts internally without specifying the areas of responsibility. This meant it was possible to give the appointee a choice of responsibilities, depending on their expertise. On one occasion, when I had been turned down for a permanent scaled post, I then had to take on some of the responsibilities which the appointee was not capable of doing, as well as showing her the ropes.

I was timetabled to teach typing, in which I have no training, for a third of my time, and I began to wonder whether they were trying to demoralise me and get me to leave the department. I wasn't far from the truth. I later discovered that I had been identified as a surplus or TAANed (Teacher Above Authorised Number) teacher and was marked for redeployment to another school. I was not last in – the four people who came in after me had all been promoted, so their jobs were safe – but I was certainly first out.

Frustrated in my aspirations and constantly undermined, I moved to a school in north London, only to experience a similar situation. On this occasion, I decided not to wait in the vain hope that things would improve and, remembering the advice of my inspector, moved into the Advisory Service; not multi-cultural education but in the area of sex discrimination. Yet I was still unhappy with the situation in which I found myself. As this was a secondment and I was still on a scale 1, I found myself in the strange position of advising schools throughout the Authority on equal opportunities issues while the renumeration I received was not commensurate with either the workload or the responsibility of the post. My counterparts in other authorities had main scale posts, as did most advisory teachers in the ILEA. Although I was glad that being a scale 1 teacher did not preclude my appointment, I felt that I did not have the status to carry out my duties effectively; so I left the Authority.

I have often wondered what life in school is like for black pupils when, as a teacher, I found myself so powerless.

The Go-Between

Gulay Mehmet

Hackney's Education Liaison Officer, Gulay Mehmet, went to Peckham Girls' School and Southwark College. She has been employed by the ILEA ever since and has worked as a teacher in Tower Hamlets and Southwark.

What is the Turkish-speaking community's experience of the ILEA? Has the Authority implemented policies which have paved the way for long-term changes? Will it be significantly missed? I will look at these questions from the perspective of my personal experience of it, which began as a pupil in Bermondsey.

I arrived in England at the age of seven, speaking only Turkish. I can only remember not being able to speak English during the first few days of junior school. I enjoyed my time there and the fact that I have no memories of learning English shows, perhaps, that it was a painless experience.

Although, on the whole, I have positive memories of secondary school, I still remember, with great clarity, wondering on my first day why I and the Afro-Caribbean girl sitting next to me were the only non-English pupils in the class, and why almost all the other Turkish and Afro-Caribbean girls were in 1a and 1m. We were soon to learn that we were in the "top stream" and "a" and "m" were the bottom streams. With the same clarity I can remember being described on many occasions as a 'nice girl' who would 'not go far academically'. I was also told that I was wasting my time

considering 'A' levels. The Afro-Caribbean girls in the lower
streams were seen as "pushy", "aggressive" and "argumentative"
by the teachers, whereas we were "quiet" and "polite". I recall
being told constantly what good mothers we would make!

The fact that we spoke another language and had experience of
another culture did not feature in the life of the school. In fact,
most of us learnt very quickly that if we wanted to be popular and
succeed we had to reject, or be seen to reject, all things that were
not English or Western and therefore not "modern" and
"civilised". For most of us this meant rejecting our first language
and the cultural values of our parents. My knowledge of two
cultures became a confining experience instead of a positive and
enriching one; at school our culture and language were ignored,
and at home our newly-acquired English culture was treated with
suspicion. I resented my parents telling my brother, my sisters
and myself to speak Turkish at home. I remember thinking,
'Turkish is not an important language, English is much more
important!' Very little in either the curriculum or pastoral care
helped us to make sense of the reality of our situation, and the
subjects offered to us were loaded with every conceivable racist
and sexist stereotype. Our futures were seen to be an arranged
marriage and children; or, for the "brighter" girls, clerical work
followed by an arranged marriage and children. There was never
any mention of such things as respect for other people's culture or
the importance of a child's mother tongue for her cognitive
development, self-realisation, cultural identity and confidence. It
was only with the support and encouragement of a very special
teacher that I developed the confidence to seriously consider a
university education.

I returned to the ILEA in the early eighties to teach in a boys'
secondary school. Eighty percent of the children were bilingual,
but on the whole it was left to a few isolated teachers to work on
anti-racist and anti-sexist issues. I found that little had changed
since my own school days.

In October 1988, only eighteen months before abolition, I joined
the ILEA's Education Liaison Service as the Liaison Officer for
Hackney. What struck me initially was how good it felt to be
working with colleagues who were from different sections of the
black community. It was also reassuring to see black people in
senior positions, but again the Turkish-speaking community was

under-represented.

I quickly discovered that being unpopular with the Authority's institutions is very closely linked to the work of a liaison officer. When I contact schools and colleges on behalf of black parents and students I am often asked why they are bringing in an "outsider". Most of the complaints I deal with concern racial harassment (both physical and verbal) and the underachievement of pupils. This shows that schools and colleges have a long way to go in establishing anti-racist practices. However, the ILEA's equal opportunities policies have generated much discussion and positive action in several areas. White staff in the Authority have been forced to address the issue of racism, no matter how uncomfortable it has made them feel.   Through the funding of Community Education Projects and language classes the ILEA has, to some extent, enabled black and bilingual students to value and sustain their mother tongues. The funding of youth projects, especially for young women, has helped provide support for Turkish children in their attempts to reconcile the demands of two different cultures.

Most recently, the ILEA's response to the Kurdish refugees issue has been prompt and sensitive, setting a positive example, not just to the new borough education services, but to local education authorities nationwide. All this work has been important.

Organising on the Ground

Amina Patel

Amina Patel is a lecturer at a college of further education and has worked for the ILEA for fifteen years. She is a founder member of Women in Sync, a women's video project.

Sixteen years ago: I was the only black student doing teaching practice in Sussex. Staff sniggered when I told them I was an English teacher. I applied to various educational authorities but I was only offered one interview, at an Islington secondary school. As a probationary teacher I was given the usual introduction to school life; I was the form tutor for a third year class and was expected to teach office skills, even though my only experience was a week's employment in an insurance brokers.

Before Channel 4, the films available to the public were limited to the kind that are on at the local Odeon. One of the more interesting tasks I undertook during that time was working with sixth formers on a film studies course jointly organised by the ILEA and the British Film Institute. My students relished a new discipline which raised debates about the power of the visual image. In the section of the course entitled "Star System" the students were critical of the fact that the hero and heroine were always white men and women. This criticism covered the vast selection of films in the ILEA Film Library. Now ILEA media studies courses include an examination of the Indian and Chinese film industries and some of the best documentaries and film stocks for educational use in the world.

My interest in the production of educational material led me to apply for a job as a Media Resource Officer (MRO). This job can have a tremendous impact in a school and plays an important role in the reception of information and the quality of learning. Of about 400 MROs, two of us were black women. There were a few more black men holding the position, but the alarming story of being overlooked for promotion was repeated, as well as the history of being placed in difficult situations with little or no support.

A black MRO's group was formed which met regularly for a year and received support from the newly created Equal Opportunities Unit. Among our concerns were the low numbers of black staff attracted and kept, conditions of work and the lack of career development. We made little headway. The contribution Andria Marsh and I made to the MRO Women's Group and the Anti-Racist Group was far more successful. On reflection, I wonder whether a group of black workers organising autonomously was just too threatening for the management to deal with.

Since race and gender issues were not addressed in the MRO's general training, we proposed that they be included in an in-service course for MROs on the assessment of existing teaching materials and the production of anti-racist teaching material. The course was well attended and we had useful feedback. However, our efforts to hold a second course were blocked by senior management after severe disagreements over who should control it.

In 1979, my move to the Resource Centre for Asian Studies, based at the Centre for Urban Educational Studies (CUES), gave me a tremendous opportunity to work with multi-ethnic co-ordinators, lecturers and teachers throughout the ILEA. On one occasion the sociologist Adarsh Sood and myself were invited to speak at a conference on "Equal Opportunities for Boys and Girls", organised for equal opportunities post-holders. We were the only black speakers and of the 112 participants only four of us were black. During the conference we discovered that race was not considered in any of the nursery, junior or secondary group discussions. We had asked the organisers to advise speakers on the importance of an anti-racist perspective, but instead found negative remarks being made about Turkish, Greek and Rastafarian families.

The Black Women in Education Group was set up in 1984 to address issues of race and gender in a way that we felt had been lacking in the Equal Opportunities Inspectorate. The three black women Multi-Ethnic Co-Ordinators, Earla Green, Pauline Duncan and Rehana Minhas, arranged for meetings of black women educationalists in their divisions, and the work of the group culminated in the 1984 Race and Gender Conference held at Isledon Teachers' Centre. It covered four main areas: community links; stereotyping; achievement; and monitoring. The response was overwhelming:-

'I enjoyed a course set up by black women without any white paternalism';

'The main speakers, Wilmette Brown and Aydin Mehmet Ali, were awe-inspiring';

'It was of historical significance.'

My last job at the Cockpit Arts Workshop has now been liquidated, along with the Youth Arts Practice which began over twenty years ago. The purpose-built theatre was host to many productions, often staged by young, inexperienced performers who learnt how to present their work to an audience in a supportive theatre environment.

I still have many criticisms of the ILEA, but I believe its abolition is a callous political act because it destroys so much of what we have all worked for.

Students

Growing up

Nicola Williams

Childhood

I shall make this child intelligent
– now, there is no excuse.

'Liberal' white neighbours, on seeing child in pram:
'Oh, what a cute little coloured baby
cootchie, cootchie, coo. Oh look, it's clapping its hands.
See how it jumps up and down ...'

They speak as if the child reminds them of something in Regent's
Park Zoo.

At Junior School:
'Wog! Sambo!'
Or the more 'well brought up' ones say
'Chocolate face ...'
'Now dear, don't say that – that's not nice
It's not his fault he's darker than us ...'

Teachers to Parents:
'...and as your son seems so withdrawn and introverted Mr and
Mrs Black (Freudian slip on his part), I don't think he is fitting in
well here. I think it's best, don't you, if he is moved to a school
suited for, er ...
boys like him ...'
(That is, an ESN school).

In Middle School – Headmaster to Parents:
'...and, as a result, I think it would be better if your son tried for the CSE examinations instead – it's no use trying for the GCE when he is not capable of doing it. But I see your son is a very outdoors type of person – Oh yes, he just loves being on the sports field you know. He's wasting his time here – he should become an athlete. Well, there'll be plenty of time for sports in his group – and there'll be many of his...er, friends there.'
(ie 80% of the school's Black children)

High School:- Careers Teacher:
either – 'Well, you've got 4 grade 3 CSEs.
Those are good grades – you can easily get a job as...er...'

or (to the 'O level ones')
'So you want to be a *doctor?*
Well perhaps, but what about becoming a nurse? I feel it would suit your caring nature so much more...'

Job Interview:- Prospective Employer:
'Do you know the job went before you arrived? Tell you what, as soon as a vacancy turns up, it's yours. Meanwhile, I believe they want ticket collectors down at the bus depot...'
But he still calls 'Next Please'.

Policemen to unemployed youth on the corner:
'What are you doing? Thinking of snatching someone's purse, are you? You Black bastards get all the luck, don't you? We don't have free time to waste. Alright I'm taking you in on 'SUS'. You look just like the other coon reported in a mugging last night. I bet I'll make that charge stick.'

What can I do?
The older ones pray – the younger ones play
I see 'Long hot summers' of the 1980s
Violence hangs in the air
Like the mushroom cloud of an H-bomb
The countdown has begun.

I weep.

Blackness is not only a Skin Colour

Andrea Williams

At my secondary school we were encouraged to take an active interest in our culture, to the extent that our teachers encouraged us to write Patois stories in the English lessons. This we thought was good at the time, but then realised that the whole point of being able to write Patois stories and poems was irrelevant if we were being examined by the traditional English exam system; something was obviously wrong. I think that we should be encouraged to take an interest in our culture, but not necessarily to the point of writing Patois in school as we are not judged on who can achieve the best broken English, but who can achieve the best standard English. Another battle that we had in my school was to allow girls who had the ability to study towards 'O' levels rather than CSEs. Unfortunately, we did not win this battle.

To know one's culture is very important as knowing the past can help to determine the future, avoiding past mistakes again. Roots and culture are transmitted to me in everyday life. I live in Brixton, one of the so-called ghetto areas of London (note that wherever black people choose to live in large numbers, is referred to as a ghetto). I listen to mostly reggae roots music, and have been reading black literature since the age of twelve.

Some youths have taken to more culturally oriented ways of life, such as the religion "Rastafarianism" which originates from Ethiopia. Because of their outward display of their roots and culture they are often stereotyped as "troublemakers" and "layabouts", their dreadlocks are seen as the most outward display of their religious beliefs and doctrines. However, unfortunately, among the black community as well as among the white community their dreadlocks are often interpreted as something "disgusting" and is seen as a "disgrace". But are dreadlocks any different from a Jew wearing his skull-cap or a Sikh wearing his turban? How else can a black person outwardly display their culture apart from locksing up their hair? Even though a person does not choose to locks his/her hair, that still does not mean that they do not sympathise or follow the Rastafarian doctrines.

Consciousness is not something that strikes someone immediately. Personally, I think you tend to become more conscious as you become more hardened to the system, and understand how tough it is for the black person to reach unlimited heights in his chosen career, even though he has the ability to succeed. To be black and conscious is of increasing importance in today's society. I say today's because on the one hand we are being told that we have equal opportunities and if we have the ability to succeed we can. Yet, while we are being told these things the government introduces the Nationality Bill which attempts to take away our birthright. Meanwhile, the Labour Party tends to portray the image of being the party for the people, which demands equality for minorities. Yet, what black people as a whole have to realise is that both major political parties are just as racist as each other. When the Deptford fire, the Colin Roach affair and the Richard "Cartoon" Campbell incidents occurred did the political parties bat an eyelid – NO! This is why it is so important for black people to be conscious, not only for their own sake now, but for the future generations also.

Blackness is not only a skin colour, it is culture and conscious-ness. Blackness is the colour of my skin, by which I will always be labelled, but my colour is rich in memories and hopes for the future. My blackness evokes my culture and my conscious-ness to the extent that I feel angry that such an intelligent race of people can be abused to such an extent, but black people must first unite in order for anything constructive to be achieved in this society.

The Missing Dimension

Jenneba Sie Jalloh

I know there will be some people who will condemn me and not want to read this, and I can't say I blame them. Some of them because they just don't care and don't see it as an issue, and others because they feel that I'm wrong in talking about us in a way that separates us from our black brothers and sisters. They may feel that this can only be detrimental and that we are black and should only talk about ourselves in the black context. I understand this (those closest to me prefer me to forget the subject or pretend it doesn't exist, but it does). You see it would be wrong of me, a lie in fact, to talk about my feelings and experiences only within the black context, what's more: impossible. In fact I've had more experiences and done more thinking as a consequence of being of mixed parents than as a consequence of being black. My feelings go beyond this. This struck me when I began to read black literature, especially that written by black American women. I found that there was something missing. I could identify with what they said, but there was still something missing, I call it *The Missing Dimension.*

I may be accused on a further count, namely; that what I am

saying is invalid. I would refute this by saying that I have feelings and emotions that some might call invalid, but the very fact that I am a human being makes them valid. However, when I thought about this more closely I realised the hypocrisy involved. There have been many times when I felt that my feelings were not important, I've even felt guilty about them. I have been more than once interrupted while reading my poem, "A Subtle Shade of Black" and told; you mustn't feel like that, or that it's wrong. But I do feel like that. I can't say whether it's right or not, but I can't and won't suppress my feelings. I know what Sam Greenlee, the author of *The Spook Who Sat By The Door,* meant when he said that a black man with a mop and bucket is invisble to white people. I feel the same way with my brothers and sisters. So long as I stay out of the limelight and out of the way; keep my feelings to myself, I will be invisible, maybe even accepted. But I won't be invisible. I don't have bogus or invalid feelings, they are the feelings of a person who feels something is wrong. If I were Jewish, Jamaican or Chinese, if I were a working-class woman, or even a middle-class white woman, if I were writing about what it feels like to be a black woman living in Britain, I would be applauded and supported. People would listen and appreciate, but few want to hear the feelings and painful experiences of a person with mixed parents. My experiences are no less painful, my feelings no less valid, but they are less straightforward, they make some people feel uncomfortable. But what is more, there is no straightforward clear-cut answer. It is personal rather than public, people can't rally round in support of my cause. What's the right response? The answer: no response. The answer is to ignore my cry, tell me that my feelings are invalid and shouldn't be voiced.

At college I tried to begin a Black Book Club. I received varied responses. Some were good, a few people appreciated what I was trying to do, but the majority wanted to know why I was doing it. Why was this "half-caste" girl trying to get people to read black literature? Was she trying to prove that she was black? (I received one such remark from a so-called friend, a friend no longer.) I had many enlightening experiences that year at college. In the room where we kept the books, we also kept a jar to collect money for the Ethiopian Fund. The money in the jar was pretty low, so one lunchtime I decided that if people wouldn't come to me, I would go to the people and thought a good place to start would be the canteen. I felt people eating would give more generously to people who are starving, and I was right. Everybody gave money and I collected about £30 that lunchtime. The response to me was different. People just could not work out why I was collecting it. Well if any of them had bothered to ask me, I could have told them it was because nobody else was. But the experience that prompted me to write "A Subtle Shade of Black" was a conversation I had one day with a sister.

She had come because she was curious and a little (no, a lot) cynical. Perhaps, it wasn't just that one occasion, but the culmination of many like it. This one was the one that broke the camel's back. There may be some people asking themselves why I am bothering to write about such a conversation with such a person. I can only say that a person can only write about what affects them as a human being. I can only write about what I know. There are some, not many, black people who feel mixed relationships are wrong, (I won't comment on this) this sister was one of them. These people feel that because "we" are products of such human relationships, that they can justifiably direct their anger or hostility against us. This sister (presuming I would know) asked me why white women went out with black men. I asked her why she thought I would know, I told her I was a black woman who went out with black men (and one in particular) and that I knew as much as her. I told her that I happened to be in this world for probably the same reason she was, namely, that my parents loved each other.

My father is black and Muslim, my mother is white and Catholic. I am neither Muslim nor Catholic. I say this because I am trying to explain, I am the result of my parents' love. I love them both very much, but I can only be responsible in that way, for myself. I want to be seen for what I am, not for what my parents are or the colour of their skin. I am black, I may be lighter than some and darker than others, but being black is not the shade of colour you are, but a state of mind, a feeling inside. I won't be anybody's scapegoat. To get back to the sister with the problem. She continued to tell me that I didn't even look black. What part of me, she asked, was black?; looking at my long hair and my light complexion. Yes, perhaps I should have ignored her, but I tried at the time to defend myself. I'm so used to trying to

defend myself that it has become a habit, but like most habits it's
becoming tiresome.

That night I thought hard and long. My thoughts were
confused. The only way I can attempt to describe the way I felt is
by writing here the poem I got that night. It came straight from
the heart, it's not contrived or edited, as I thought it and felt it, I
wrote it, word for word. As I wrote the last three words I couldn't
see what I had written.

A Subtle Shade of Black (identity unknown)

There is so much going on inside me
I am mixed up, I am confused
I have no name, no country, no home, no colour
I am ME, but what am I?
Is to be oneself enough, or does one need more?
To fight for a cause and to be shunned by those
you fight for as not belonging to them
Who then? Where then must I go? Who do I belong to?

A spiteful word, a slip of the tongue, a cover up;
RED BITCH – OUTSIDER

Never one or the other
Fighting to be one, Wanting to be one, Needing to be one
But scared. Always there, but never there
Who am I? What am I? Where do I belong?

Always wanting, but never daring
I, always talking, but never quite believing
They, always accepting, but never quite believing
Never quite accepting
Proud of my colour, but never quite sure if I am allowed to be
Never quite sure of my right to be
ARE YOU LAUGHING AT ME?
I am Black, I am a sister
YOU ARE HALFCASTE
I am Black
YOU ARE HALFCASTE
I am halfcaste

SORROW
PAIN
DIVISION

There is a consistency about my feelings and ideas, and that is they fluctuate enormously. In the past two years I have experienced a vast range of emotions from feeling black, disliking white people and wanting to find my roots, to feelings of lack of identity and disliking of black people for treating me like an outsider, to believing that all people are the same regardless of skin colour, and a few months ago I came to the conclusion that no black person including my closest friends truly, deep down believed I am black. Then I told myself that I would fight for any oppressed people whatever their colour of skin. These are some of the emotions I have experienced and continue to experience. There is only one thing I know, and that is that I will be involved in the struggle, in whatever way I can, primarily for my people, and if at any stage during my life I experience an identity crisis because I am told by my people that I do not belong (as has happened before) I will know anyway and be confident at least that I am fighting for my fellow human beings. A sad compromise maybe, but I, unlike my brothers and sisters' cannot ignore what my heart and my mind are saying to me, or the attacks on my identity.

In a way I'd like to finish on a positive note, but I am not going to, not because I can't – I will continue to fight and feel for my black sisters and brothers whether they like it or not, or whether they accept me as one of them or not, I've managed this far even though sometimes it hurts and is far from easy. I won't because I don't want anyone to walk away feeling comfortable thinking that I've got it worked out. I still have two fights; my public one and my private one, the one with my people which they force upon me, and the one for them. I will leave you with this; when I was four years old I asked my mother this question: 'Mummy am I black?', the matter-of-fact way I asked her took her aback. It was simply the question of a small child, asked with the frankness and simplicity of a young, enquiring mind. What she supposed to be a simple straightforward question? 'Mummy am I black', I first asked the question when I was four years old, I am twenty now, sixteen years later I'm still asking the same question and I still don't really know the answer. Maybe because nobody really knows or maybe because nobody really wants to.

If this essay has left you feeling confused with the feeling that whoever wrote it must be in a similar confused state of mind, you

160

AGAINST THE TIDE

may be right.

(For my Mum and Dad who made me rich; I love them and thank them always).

Extra School

The Black Supplementary School Movement

Winston Best

Winston Best is the Senior Inspector for Education in Hackney

S upplementary schools are organised learning arrangements which Afro-Caribbean people in Britain have established in their communities as a way of supporting the social learning experience of their children. In the main, these schools meet for about two hours on Saturday mornings, though some meet after school during weekdays or on Sundays. Other minority communities also organise educational activities at the weekend for their children. However, these tend to be classes concerned with the teaching of the mother tongue to bilingual children mainly from the Asian subcontinent, although also from Europe and North Africa. As the number of black families increased in the United Kingdom during the fifties and sixties the need for educational support for their children became apparent. This led parents to seek private tuition for their children – a practice that is prevalent in the Caribbean. In London, the beginnings of organised supplementary education can be traced back to the early sixties. Almost contemporaneously three groups of black adults living in Shepherds Bush, Haringey and Islington began working with young children of Afro-Caribbean origin. The work began around 1964 and the individuals in each group shared at least one thing in common – they were all members of the West Indian Standing Conference (WISC), a social organisation formed in 1959 following the Notting Hill disturbances.

In 1968 the supplementary school movement received a big boost. Following a successful campaign to persuade Haringey Education Authority to abandon their plans for banding and distributing black pupils across the borough, a new organisation concerned only with education was formed, the Caribbean Education Community Workers' Association (CECWA). CECWA campaigned vigourously to draw the plight of black children in British schools to the attention of the education authorities, particularly the disproportionate number found to be attending schools for the educationally subnormal (ESN). To boost its campaign, CECWA collaborated with Bernard Coard to publish the pamphlet *How The West Indian Child Is Made Educationally Sub-normal In The British Education School System*. This publication was used to launch a national campaign for the creation of black supplementary schools and black parents' groups, particularly in those urban areas where the Afro-Caribbean community formed a sizeable part of the population. The success of this campaign was phenomenal and it established permanently the black supplementary school movement as a serious pressure group for educational change in the British education system.

The black supplementary school movement has five specific aims:

(1) To help new arrivals to the United Kingdom from the Caribbean settle easily into their family situation, their new schools and their local environment.

(2) To ensure that young Afro-Caribbeans learn about their cultural heritage.

(3) To provide extra tuition in the three Rs for school students.

(4) To offer educational advice and support to parents of Afro-Caribbean children.

(5) To campaign for better and more relevant education for children of Afro-Caribbean origin in the British education system.

The black supplementary school movement has grown in character, confidence and influence over the years as the schools have gained local and national recognition. The ILEA's response is characteristic of that in the rest of the country. In 1978, following the publication of the ILEA's policy on multi-ethnic education, the senior officers took a decision to advise Members that they should recognise officially the work of these schools and offer them a modicum of financial support. As a consequence, a limited number of grants were made available to the schools and the Multi-Ethnic Inspectorate was asked to establish formal links with them. Twelve schools were supported at first. This number has now risen to about twenty. There are a number of conditions placed on grant aid.

1. The schools should be viable institutions.
2. They should cater for children living in the ILEA.
3. They should keep proper accounts.
4. They should liaise with the Multi-Ethnic Inspectorate.

The support offered by the ILEA could hardly be considered as more than token. It permitted the supplementary schools to do little more than to pay the travelling expenses of some of its teachers and helpers and to purchase materials for the pupils to use. For some, however, this was a welcome relief from a few of the financial pressures under which they were operating. For others it was a struggle with their conscience. The acceptance of grant aid from public funding bodies has always been a controversial issue. Since the aid is inevitably granted with strings attached, community members have always regarded this as something to avoid at all cost since it hampers their operating style. They have to avoid publicly criticising their funding agents and if the institution has charitable status it has to avoid being overtly involved in political campaigns. No supplementary school worth its salt can afford not to be political. It is dealing with a situation that is embarrassing to the education authorities. The very existence of the movement is an indication of the failure of the state education system to satisfy the needs of the pupils and parents.

In some ways the black officers who were involved in the consultation process over funding for these schools were able to make the ILEA funding officers aware of these fears and sensitive to the kinds of demands which they were making of the groups. Hence, minimum accountability was agreed. It would be foolish, however, to think that it was all plain sailing between these schools and the ILEA. Many of them had a tough time convincing some administration officers that they were not only genuine organisations but that they were responsible and capable of administering sums of money, however small. Frequently the intervention of a black officer was necessary to convince officers that the groups could be trusted. This is not the time to be overcritical of how the ILEA viewed these organisations but there can be little doubt that there was a general feeling among the supplementary schools that they were treated differently from white voluntary organisations and that it may have had something to do with institutional racism.

For many of the black supplementary school workers, anti-racism is perceived as no more than a continuation of the struggle for equal rights and equal opportunities in all aspects of their lives. Anti-racism is not only about struggling to remove racist barriers to achievement, it is also about exposing actions, however well meaning, that are disadvantageous to an already beleaguered black minority. Black anti-racism, therefore, may at times take on a different meaning and dimension from that of white anti-racism. Sometimes they may well be in conflict with each other. There are times when anti-racism appears to have a "filling of the begging bowl" image; it is acceptable if it does not pose a threat to the white power base. This explains why it is possible to have many black workers doing menial jobs but few in positions of real power. It explains why so few black governors are still on governing bodies; it explains why so few black people are in senior positions in the schools and in administration; it explains why the competition for posts in schools above a certain level becomes such a fierce power struggle.

Anti-racism has to be seen in terms of making opportunities available to all, commensurate with their skills, knowledge and potential contribution to the development of the society as a whole. It is not working if, in a society where many people come from a particular ethnic group, these people are hardly represented in the workforce at a level above that of the cleaners. A future role for the black supplementary school movement must, therefore, be to act as a monitoring agent of the outcomes of anti-racist policies in all institutions. Theirs will have to be a campaigning role for greater achievement of black pupils in schools and more realistic promotion for black teachers in the system. They will have to be very clear about how far they will wish to support certain white power bases who, by their actions, undermine the struggle to succeed.

The passing of the ILEA will make the task more difficult for those of us who operate in the London area since we will have to deal with many more individual borough councils. There is therefore a greater need for co-ordination of the supplementary school movement to ensure that the struggle can be carried on successfully on several fronts. One legacy for the black movement after the death of the ILEA should be a properly constituted and funded umbrella organisation for the black supplementary schools. We will miss the ILEA and the pioneering work which it has done. What we must not do is lay down arms and give up the fight.

ILLYAH

Roz Howell

Roz Howell is Director of Equal Opportunities at Greenwich Community Relations Council.

He is underachieving. What do you mean, lady? It took nine months to make this child. It took just five years to potty train him, teach him to count and say his prayers, tell the time, write his name, brush his teeth and comb his hair for himself. He has learnt to scale Mt Everest, drive through Brands Hatch and do more daring things than Batman and Robin, and now you tell me he is understimulated after six years in your care. You were the gateway to achievement. What do you mean it's my fault he won't learn? Why don't you knock the daylights out of him, I mean whack him, he know he has to learn. What do you mean, you can't? You are his teacher, why don't you teach him, twice one are two, twice two are four?

Where I come from the only people who can't read are those who don't get the chance to go to school. What do you mean I am Victorian and that is old-fashioned? That was good enough for me, why isn't it good enough for him?

When I taught him to count he knew his numbers. What did you do to him? Oh, now I see, you didn't want your hand to touch him, you frightened of him. Aren't you the teacher? How come you 'fraid the child? You know the child cannot spell his name, he cannot even tell if it's a 53 or 108 bus, but he knew that when he came to school. No, I don't see the child is educationally subnormal. I better see the head.

Good morning. Miss What's-her-name tells me the child is uneducable. No one in my family had that problem before. In fact, my brother Boysie who works for British Rail used to be a headmaster. My sister is a doctor and all her children are in high school; her first has just been admitted to university, so what is wrong with this school?

I hear you do not beat the knowledge into the children. ILLYAH say you cannot wallop them, you have to stick to the curriculum. They didn't have no curriculum where I come from, so you think I should go back, he might do better? No, they do not live in trees over there, and we do not have steel band music for breakfast; in fact, my father absolutely forbade calypso. We used to play Beethoven and Bach on the piano. Yes, really.

Do tell me more about ILLYAH. Oh, she doesn't actually know every child but she is responsible, she with the government. Oh, she is not a she, ILEA is the Inner London Education Authority, who determine policy for education.

So how come the children are under, what did you say, you mean they not learning, why don't you try my way? He learn a lot of things when I used to teach him. Oh, so it's my fault, your way is better, so how come he ain't learning? I think I had better speak to the child.

Woman, what you stropping for?

I can strops if I want to. You remember I went to see his teacher? Well I feel so bad, she stood there in she posh accent and tell me the child is an underachiever. No matter how much I try to get her to break his back, she keep telling me ILLYAH, they don't beat learning into children, they expect them to learn through activity.

He is active enough, you should talk to the child. You go to all those meetings and you own child can't read.

Child, come here, Saturday bright and early you going to the Supplementary School. Stop screwing you face up. No cinema. No walking the streets. Look, I did not take nine months to bring an underachiever into the world. What will your aunt say when she hear you are an underachiever? You don't care? I do, England is good for education; Shakespeare and Winston Churchill, all of them read. What you mean, they white? Well, Marcus Garvey, Luther King, Nelson Mandela, they could read. What do you mean their teacher didn't call them nigger and wog and sunshine? Who call you that? Nice lady is only concern about you, she won't even hit you. Don't let me have to wake you. I getting up five o'clock to clean and do the washing, then you have to have breakfast and down we go.

Good morning Miss, the boy is twelve and he can't read. What do you mean, don't blame him?

That woman is good boy, she want more of us in County Hall to tell them how we want our children taught. Well I dey wid that! I do not care how tired I am.

How long this ILEA running? How come I never heard of it? Well, I don't care how long it takes, we will show them how to teach our children.

After all that work we get two of them in there, one Indian, one Afro-Caribbean. The work was worth it – what did the big white one say? We have an Equal Opportunity Policy, we need more black teachers, we need role models and soon the black child will not underachieve. Parents will be able to go into school and partake in their children's learning, they will decide the curriculum.

What you doing home so early boy? What you mean, suspended? The teacher want to see me? What I going for she, let she tell me you are an underachiever! I will give she underachiever. You teacher on Saturday say you are bright boy.

Good morning. Behavioural problems? What kind of behavioural problems? He is lippy. How lippy? You ask him to pray for Terry Waite and he want to pray for Nelson Mandela. I have to keep him home. But who is going to teach him? He has his 'O' levels next month.

This time you gone too far. Yes, I will be there at your meeting, and me husband too and all the people from the race place. You think Equal Opportunity is about women. Well, let me tell you it is about race equality too. You, an you are a bloody racist! You can exclude him if you wish, it is your right but I will see you roast in Hell. My son will have a degree, with or without you. Yes, I am going to complain to ILEA. All you sorry, my son will have to make other arrangements for his education. White people are heartless, except Joan.

What you say? They abolishing ILEA? You going to march? Well, I ain't missing that! Thatcher ain't going to get away with it. As for Baker, he don't even know what a dozen is, he still think it is thirteen. We can't let them take over education, they don't know nothing. ILEA paid for the Supplementary School, it's not their fault that good-for-nothing blackman ran away with the money. Anyway, Thatcher is only shutting it down because a blackman is going to be head. Whatever happen to that first black woman who brought us all to County Hall? They kicked her out? I think she running a restaurant now.

ILEA Sponsored Projects

The Afro-Caribbean Resource Project

Len Garrison

The Afro-Caribbean Education Resource Project (ACER) produced much of the anti-racist learning material currently in use in Britain's schools. More recently the ACER's work has been translated for use in schools in the Netherlands. This historic account highlights the significant impact that a small, independent educational resource and publishing unit had, working in partnership with the ILEA between 1978 and 1988. Len Garrison is the ACER's former Director and co-founder.

Looking back after thirteen years, ACER's growth seems like an almost impossible feat. Having started, in a basement in Stockwell, as a small group concerned about the lack of resolution to the crisis that faced black children in schools, Paul Boateng and I decided to take up the challenge by becoming co-founders of ACER. Our philosophy was that schools should be made to work for all pupils. Black children should not have to go outside the mainstream schools to seek recognition and gain confidence in being themselves. White pupils should also learn about being black in a white society. Together pupils could learn to respect each other.

This was to be achieved by a positively created multi-cultural environment and purpose-designed learning resources. The experiment was to challenge the then popular assimilationist Eurocentric model of education, more commonly called the "colour-blind" approach, which informed most educational practice. The plan was to devise a major Afro-Caribbean library resource base as well as develop a programme of materials which identified the ethnic, cultural and social dimensions of the black child, acknowledging them as an integral part of learning for all pupils.

This programme was developed as a community response to underachievement. It was a countermeasure against the identification by the authorities of black children as the cause of their own problem – namely, being black, being of a different culture, and just being different. A local newspaper pointed to one of the real factors, as identified by Professor Alan Little in a lecture at the time:

> Lack of action by Government in schools could mean that a second generation of black youngsters is being launched on a vicious downward spiral of deprivation. (South London Press, 11.3.78).

This explanation of black underachievement had come about because of various factors. One was the publication of Bernard Coard's experience and testimony as a teacher in a school for educationally subnormal (ESN) children in the booklet *How the West Indian Child is made Educationally Subnormal in the British School System.*[1]

A second factor was the publication of the Bullock Report, *A Language for Life,*[2] which acknowledged the need for a positive approach to tackling the question of linguistic diversity and multi-ethnic education. The report argued convincingly 'that a child should not have to leave its culture or language at the door of the school.' But how change was to come about and who should take up the challenge to make this a reality was an open question.

Meanwhile, black parents could not see any resolution to the problems their children faced in school in terms of overt and covert racism. By the end of the seventies supplementary schools had sprung up in many communities as a way of helping enhance black pupils' education and compensating for the lack of cultural support and the mis-education in the schools.

A few schools did try to make up the deficit in the curriculum and developed a black studies package for black children in the lower stream as a way of appeasing critics who saw schools as indifferent to black pupils' needs. It was Maureen Stone in her book *The Education of the Black Child in Britain – The Myth of Multi-racial Education*[3] who argued that racism was the problem rather than black children's culture. These assertions that the black child, family and culture were not responsible for wholesale underachievement helped to prepare the way for ACER's schemes. Equally the focus on countering racism as an integral part of combating underachievement gained currency.

In 1977, when the ILEA passed its first multi-ethnic policy document, ACER was included as a partnership project. The ACER scheme sought to produce learning materials, based on classroom trials, which would bring the everyday experiences of the black child into the mainstream classroom activity. It also sought to develop and gather together into a central bank a range of curriculum materials from various souces relating to the Afro-Caribbean and black British experiences. These were to act as a source of reference for classroom teachers and others pursuing a more positive approach to multi-cultural education. This specialist collection eventually became the largest independent collection of books and non-book sources, not only in the ILEA area, but in the country as a whole.

ACER's structure and its relationship with the local authority was a unique one. Although ACER established itself as an independent educational charity, it was devised on a partnership basis between the black community and the ILEA. The management committee comprised teachers, parents, school governors and community workers representing community interests. Officers of the Multi-Ethnic Inspectorate, namely Bev Woodroffe and Mike Hussey, also played an important part in their advisory role and in liasion between ACER and the Authority.

ACER's primary goal in its first phase was the designing, developing and piloting of new materials, set out in its programme. These were to offer teachers an opportunity to start from where the children were and incorporate the multi-cultural content into the mainstream school curriculum in order to improve the quality of education on offer to all pupils.

During this phase of development a multi-disciplinary team of five staff worked in cramped conditions in an area twenty feet square at the ILEA's Centre for Learning Resources. The team comprised a School Liaison Officer, a Research Officer, a Director, a Graphic Designer/Illustrator and an Administrative Officer. Production of resources involved piloting materials in a number of schools and running in-service evaluation sessions with teachers.

This period saw the publication of the *Ourselves* pack, which was based on stories of a group of children from various backgrounds celebrating their differences, and the piloting of

Words and Faces, a pack to help children develop their self-perceptions, image, vocabulary and use of language through drawing, colouring and discussion. Both of these units were designed for middle school (nine to fourteen years) children. Once published, there was an immediate demand for the material as teachers saw the positive results. A large part of ACER's work was a ground-breaking and pioneering role. Looking back, it achieved a remarkable amount, considering the limited size of the project, the hostile climate and the negative response from some quarters during the early period of the project's development. The team worked in a pioneering and co-operative spirit in order to effect change.

Schools which had been hesitant and even resistant began to see positive results as black children began to accept unapologetically their colour before their friends and teachers. White pupils, encouraged by ACER materials, began to accept difference in a positive way, and teachers began to feel less threatened by being asked to treat race-related issues positively.

Alongside this work, ACER initiated the annual Black Young Writers' Award, now in its eleventh year. The competition grew rapidly with entries from over 300 students nationally and the awards ceremony draws an audience of over 500 to Lambeth Town Hall, Brixton, each February.

In the second phase the project expanded to ten workers, culminating in 1985 with a move to larger accommodation and a base of its own in Wyvil School, Vauxhall in south London. Specially refurbished, the base was organised into a library to house the 7000-8000 books and the non-book collection, a graphics and print room with a complete in-house printing outfit, and a large workroom for staff.

While we were developing material for middle school pupils, a constant question from parents, under fives workers and teachers had been, 'What about the early years?' The second phase, therefore, concentrated on producing a unit of material for this age group. *I'm Special: Myself,* an introductory pack including early learning books in full colour photographs plus teachers' and parent guide to assist the three to seven year olds explore ideas about themselves, was published. Again, the strength of the materials was that they were child-centred, allowing children to start learning from where they are and encouraging them to feel positive about being different. Demands for this material was equally good, requests outstripping supplies in the first year of production.

ACER's work was enhanced by a series of videos produced by the ILEA Television Centre. *To School Together*, for instance, documents the use of ACER materials by pupils in the classroom. In *Anti-Racism in Practice*, Professor Stuart Hall examines the wider implications of such materials and the challenge they present, particularly to 'unthinking racist assumptions'. Referring to the enormous changes Britain has undergone in world relations since the Second World War, Stuart Hall raises the crucial issue of how one re-educates whole populations 'into an entirely new attitude' to cope with the realities of a multi-ethnic society. The video programme, *Multi-Culturalism in the United States* in which Professor Geneva Gay discusses the parallel development in the institutions in that country, also added an important dimension to the work of ACER. These programmes played a valuable role in highlighting and popularising the work of ACER nationally.

Throughout the history of ACER, its independent community stance meant that it could be objective and openly critical of the lack of clear action and results from ILEA's policies. My own critical review of the situation in a paper in 1985 highlighted some of the major concerns:-

> Over the past six years, the ILEA has attempted to devise a formula which would make the educational process more conducive to learning for Black and other ethnic groups in school... There has also been a clear failure to come to terms with the various forms of racism which restrict the Multi-Cultural concept of education from becoming a reality... failure also to come to terms with the magnitude of the situation and to evaluate work that has been carried out or effect changes in areas which remain untouched.

In summing up the situation, we could say that the multi-ethnic and anti-racist policies, as part of the recent equal opportunities initiatives, have been more of a paper exercise and have not been given the base or financial commitment needed to mount an effective campaign.

To place the primary focus of the funding of ACER onto its commercial viability, called for with the demise of the ILEA, immediately puts on the pressure to cut down development and research and to prioritise profit. We can only speculate at this point on the consequences. What remains certain is that all children must know who they are before they can appreciate and value others. White children receive constant affirmation from the dominant values within mainstream education. That right must be extended to all, thus making the cultural diversity of pupils a strength rather than a weakness. Positive affirmation of oneself in all curriculum resources is not only imperative for every individual, it is a right.

What significance could we attribute to the role and unique contributions made by ACER to the development of resources and anti-racist educational practice in the ILEA? Summing up in a paper presented in September 1985 to a CRE conference on "Resourcing Change", I made some suggestions:

> The work of the ACER Project has shown that pupils of the middle years of schooling can be given a more equitable start in the classroom – that learning materials do not have to be only about one point of reference. Learning can take place from and about each other while children are allowed to share their own experience...Children also show that they respect each other more when the teachers and the classroom materials support each other's point of view. The ACER learning materials have shown that they can provide an important lead in this work.[4]

Both the Rampton and Swan Reports acknowledged the need for a positive affirmation of black children's presence in British schools, thus supporting the basic tenet of ACER's challenge to Eurocentric education. The Swann Report also highlighted the importance of cultural pluralism as a contribution to the all-white school debate. Baroness Young, as the then Minister of State, talking in April 1980 at the CRE conference on education for a multi-cultural society, stated:

> It is just as important in a school where there are no ethnic minority pupils, for the teaching there to refer to the different cultures now present in Britain, as it is for the teaching in schools in the inner areas of cities like Birmingham and London. It is a question of developing a curriculum which draws positive advantage from different cultures.[5]

The mid-eighties saw much debate centring around multi-cultural education as a token gesture. ACER's contribution has, however, further challenged that stereotype of cultural diversity and produced positive curricula resources and practice. An important factor in its success nationally has been that its materials have proved equally accessible to white pupils in predominantly white schools, therefore questioning the value of Eurocentric materials with their distorted reality. However, with the demise of ILEA, ACER's future is uncertain.

Notes:
1. New Beacon Books, 1971.
2. HMSO, 1975.
3. Fontana, 1981.
4. Len Garrison, *Resources for Education in a Plural Society: Policy to Practice,* ACER, 1985.
5. Baroness Young, *Education for All: The Swann Report,* Cmnd 9453, p. 227.

The Centre for Urban Educational Studies

CUES Staff talking to Sarah Olowe

The Centre for Urban Educational Studies (CUES) is the ILEA's specialist multi-ethnic-anti-racist teachers' centre.

The Centre for Urban Educational Studies (CUES) was set up in Islington in 1963 as a specialist centre with the aim of helping teachers respond to the educational needs of the urban communities of inner London. A particular concern in the 1960s and 1970s was how teachers could develop the English language skills of an increasing number of bilingual pupils. Subsequent work in language and communication has led to a greater understanding of the importance of the language and cultural perspective of people's home and community. This is reflected in a growing national awareness of the vital relationship between schools and the inner city communities they serve. In the early seventies the Community Division of CUES was established to work on specific projects with local schools and communities, and in 1970 it started offering the only recognised in-service qualification for teaching English as a second language.*After the publication of

* In 1987 the ESL diploma was renamed Teaching Across the Curriculum in Multi-Lingual Schools to reflect the increasing awareness of racism as a factor in children's experience of education, and the move away from ESL teaching to mainstream classroom support.

AGAINST THE TIDE

the ILEA's first multi-ethnic education policy in 1979, the CUES became the only major centre in the Authority to provide anti-racist and multi-ethnic in-service training for teachers. In 1986 we moved from Whitechapel, where we had been for five years, to a larger building in Vauxhall, which is our current home.

When schoolteachers come to the Centre for our day release course their classes are covered by one of our team of teachers. CUES teachers work in four schools each week, using the fifth day for liaison with the classroom teachers who attend our course. The team have access to all the CUES resources, and they have built up a resource bank of practical teaching and learning aids. In 1988 our full team of seventeen teachers worked and supported over one hundred primary schools.

Our staff have directed training in many countries, including Colombia, Sweden, Pakistan and the Federal Republic of Germany; and yet none of the London boroughs, either singly or collectively, has decided whether to fund the CUES after the ILEA has been abolished. Instead, many London boroughs are looking to polytechnics, higher education colleges, and consultancy firms for their in-service training needs. Many of these institutions have relatively little experience of the learning needs of London's children.

The format and emphasis of the training that we offer has obviously changed over the years. It has been necesary to reflect both the ILEA's anti-racist policies and the changing demands of schools as educationalists have become more aware of the language and learning processes of children. Our staff have also changed in response to both our own anti-racist policy and the need to recruit more black and bilingual staff. One thing that has not changed, however, is the total commitment of all our staff to improving the educational achievement of the black and bilingual pupils in ILEA schools.

Working at the CUES in the Seventies

Marina Foster

Marina Foster came to England from South Africa in 1969. She studied at several British universities as a United Nations Fellow and was a permanent worker at the ILEA's Centre for Urban Educational Studies for ten years. Ms Foster is currently Co-Ordinator of Education (Racial Equality) in Berkshire.

It was exhilarating coming to London in the seventies. There were so many innovations in so many fields and the educational world was attempting to come to terms with the presence in London schools of children with special difficulties, as they were categorised in those days. It would be easy, with the wisdom of hindsight, to put a contemporary gloss on those events, but many of the principles, practices and issues that have become commonplace in the eighties were bought dearly by those of us who joined the ILEA in the seventies.

The life of a United Nations Fellow (sic) and mature student at a British liberal university masks, to a great extent, the realities of the workplace. Nothing that I recall in my previous life prepared me for my appointment to the post as tutor at the Centre for Urban Educational Studies (CUES). It took nearly six months for the Department of Education and Science to recognise my post-graduate degrees and diplomas, acquired at British universities and colleges, and to grant me the coveted QTS (qualified teacher status). But I was so keen to work in ILEA that I waited! It seemed nothing could be done; and certainly nothing that was done to hasten or influence the delay was to any avail.

Consequently I worked for many months as an uncertified teacher while holding a master's degree and two advanced diplomas in education from the University of London and the Froebel College.

The Centre for Urban Educational Studies was renowned for its open lecture series which offered London teachers training by those in the forefront of research into issues of language, culture and community concerns. I was therefore surprised when, after a complaint from a senior colleague, I was carpeted for organising the series based on the research of the authors of a book called *Between Two Cultures*! I thought I had pulled off a coup in attracting these researchers to the CUES but apparently senior workers thought that language tutors should stick to language issues. It highlighted how the internal structure of a centre like CUES had inherent contradictions which acted against the addressing of racism and underachievement in ILEA schools. On that occasion I had consulted with the "community tutor", who fully supported me in running the series, so my infringement of the internal boundaries was overlooked. In itself this may not seem important, but it is indicative of much wider concerns which surfaced gradually.

One issue concerned whether the Centre should receive visitors from South Africa. As a whole, the staff reflected the range of views and opinions found in Britain at large in the seventies. It was therefore not surprising that they wanted to maintain a dialogue with South Africa about its apartheid policies. There was only one other dissenting voice apart from my own, a young tutor who had just joined the staff. She was severely reprimanded for "interfering" in the debate, but as a compromise I was granted permission not to be on duty on the occasion of such visits.

As more black staff began to be recruited to CUES the issue of racism began to be challenged more often and more vigorously. It was encouraging when staff decided to explore the issue in a series of staff meetings devoted specifically to examining racism within the Centre and more generally. However, when I proposed that black staff should form a black caucus and that we should be excused from attending these sessions of self-analysis and consciousness raising, my colleagues were outraged. I did not see myself as a "resource" but hours of argument and discussion did not convince anyone that, as an oppressed black woman, it was neither my role nor my responsibility to facilitate the consciousness raising of my colleagues. I lost the argument and staff insisted that I be present at all the sessions. Today, if I were to adopt such a stand, my position would be unassailable. We have at last won the right to organise independently on issues that directly affect black people, although many people still do not accept its legitimacy.

In the eighties the ILEA's Multi-Ethnic Inspectorate began to have a positive effect on the proceedings at CUES, in subtle ways as well as in matters of general policy. Working to a wider brief, they were concerned about the content and quality of the whole curriculum and about the standards of attainment and the general ethos of the ILEA schools. This team's work acted as a model for the country and my involvement with it drew me out of the Centre more and more.

Later on I was given the responsibility of running one of the CUES' Inset (In-service training) courses. Despite my years of experience in teacher training it took many years before I was awarded this accolade. As many black teachers in the ILEA will recognise from their own experience, I served a very long second apprenticeship. In the year that I was asked to run the course I had branched out into many areas of work beyond material development: I had been asked to work with the Afro-Caribbean Education Resource team one day a week; I had also begun an Inset course for teachers of primary mathematics at the Polytechnic of North London to update my own professional development. Then there was also my membership of the editorial committee of the ILEA Multi-Ethnic Education Review, which had just been established. This was an exciting team who were task-oriented and a joy to work with. I also participated in the editorial meetings at the ILEA Learning Material Service (LMS), chaired jointly by the Director of LMS and the Senior Inspector for Multi-Ethnic Education. This committee of editors, teachers, tutors and curriculum developers was established to review and develop the multi-cultural perspective of the learning materials being published by the ILEA. This is one of the dimensions of the ILEA's materials that won it acclaim and ranked its materials among the best in the country. CUES in-service courses were then organised one day a week over thirty weeks in the year. This was not a heavy workload and not incompatible with all the other things I was involved in at that time. It was felt, however, that I should curtail some of my outside activities, 'for my own good'.

Being an in-service tutor and course organiser, I was in a position to attract a wide range of people to lecture and give talks to teachers to broaden their perspectives. It was possible to invite lecturers who could open up wider educational and cultural perspectives beyond the academic and practical constraints of the classroom. Most important of all, it was possible to invite speakers from community organisations and other educational establishments who could give talks from an informed and experienced viewpoint. CUES courses were planned collaboratively but there were two of us who constantly came up against opposition to our choice of speakers. It was felt that they were too critical, too outspoken or too radical and that they would antagonise the teachers coming on our courses. Partly for this reason I made it standard practice at the end of all my courses to get course members to evaluate the courses that I tutored. What emerged was that the course members were positive and enthusiastic about such speakers. They also told us that they were keen to widen their horizons and to improve their classroom practice and teaching strategies, and keen to work towards improving the educational provision in their classrooms. We know now that that is only part of the answer, but at the time their response was regarded as another step forward.

In 1982 the ILEA set up its Equal Opportunities Unit which consulted widely throughout the Authority to see whether a policy on equality of opportunities was not only desirable but necessary. Imagine my surprise when I discovered that the Centre had submitted a paper to the Unit without engaging in the usual collaborative process! Those who have read the CUES occasional paper, *Equal Opportunities; a Personal Black Perspective,* will perhaps understand the title better.

In the ten years that I worked at the Centre several scale posts were awarded but they never seemed to come in my direction. In 1982 I discovered by chance that a post was being offered internally, as usual I was not one of the internal candidates invited to apply. The discrimination in this case was too blatant to be allowed to slip by unchallenged. I referred the matter to the Caribbean Teachers' Association, of which I was a member, and I believe it was taken up at a senior level.

I left the ILEA in December 1983 to face an even bigger challenge out in the Shires. Despite everything that transpired in those ten years I feel very positive about my involvement in the educational scene, limited and as limiting as it might seem today. It was a time of tremendous personal and professional growth for me.

Among my farewell gifts were an alarm clock, a hand-woven shawl from India and a book of poems, which I value very dearly. The following quotation says it all:

And she went forth with others of her kind
to scythe the earth knowing that bondage
would not fall like a poultice from the
children's forehead
But O she grieved for them
in another land
walking beadless.

From 'One Continent/To Another'
By Grace Nicholls

Working at the CUES in the Eighties

Chiaka Amadi

Chiaka Amadi joined Stoke Newington School in 1982 to teach Spanish and French. In 1987 she was seconded to the Centre for Urban Educational Studies as an ESL advisory teacher. Ms Amadi currently works in Hackney's education planning department.

The phrase that most immediately comes to mind whenever I reflect on my seven years as an ILEA secondary school teacher is "formation of character". When I joined the Authority as a probationary teacher, though not timid, I was reserved and slightly uncertain of what to expect. I was only partially aware of what life was like for the majority of students in inner London, but was urged on by a belief in the right of every student to have access to education of the highest quality.

Oddly enough it was none of the more memorable events in my probationary year that indicated how my career would develop. It was not, for example, when some fifth-year boys kicked the door of a science laboratory off its hinges; nor the day the third years refused to have a Spanish lesson. The prophetic event happened shortly after I had been burgled twice in three days. The bottom of my front door had been sawn off in one burglary. When I expressed my distress to the headteacher I was told I should not allow my personal life to interfere with my work at school and maybe I was unsuited to teaching; an unwarranted statement in a situation where any other member of the department would have been shown some sympathy.

Subsequently I joined the ILEA's Minority Ethnic Representation Group (MERG). MERG acted a a pressure group on the Central Management Team (CMT) and represented the concerns of black and ethnic minority staff. Given the apparently progressive environment I hadn't anticipated conflict between us and the senior management. Nevertheless conflict came.

MERG lobbied the CMT to get the *ad hoc* Bengali, Turkish and Gujerati classes properly resourced and timetabled within the school day. We also took up particular cases, like the black colleague who had been told formally by his headteacher that he was preventing the development of positive anti-racist attitudes in the school because he was such a poor role model, or another black colleague who had returned from maternity leave to find her classes had been assigned to a white male supply teacher and that she was required to do cover instead. While each case we dealt with was different, poor management and plain racism were recurrent themes.

Eventually I became an advisory teacher at the Centre for Urban Educational Studies (CUES), which at the time was managed by the Multi-Ethnic Inspectorate. The CUES had a reputation for doing pioneering work, but any high expectations I had were dispelled when I found myself being systematically hindered and underminded by a small group of white, so-called "anti-racist" colleagues, who on the one hand argued that it was important to empower and involve black people, but on the other did their best to prevent black people having any control. When this group of people were challenged about their inconsistent behaviour, they justified it by saying that they understood racism because they had black friends.

The CUES was started in the early sixties but until 1987 all its directors had been white. My arrival coincided with the appointment of two black directors, and as a result of their systematic questioning, which included a review of the anti-racist policy at CUES, they came face to face with anger, resentment and hostility. Teachers were usually seconded to the CUES from their regular schools, normally for one or two years. A significant number of the CUES staff had been there for two years or more, and they became very upset when the new directors wanted to stick to the two-year rule so that other teachers could have the

AGAINST THE TIDE   193

opportunity of coming to CUES and would benefit from the career enhancement it would bring. Two white colleagues were supportive, but there was a hard core of white women teachers who did their best to undermine the new directors. The infamous phrase 'I am not a racist but...' was used on countless occasions. Again it was up to the Authority's black staff to organise the fight back.

The struggles I have described were definitely not for the faint-hearted, but, in a sense, the ILEA showed me the world. In acknowledging the debt I owe, how can I but thank and pay tribute to the various colleagues, heads of department, heads of year, senior management teams, divisional inspectors and subject inspectors who all worked hard and contributed to my achievements as an ILEA teacher. Will I forget the good example these people set, trying to give pupils and students their rights and entitlements within our education system? Never.

Further and Higher Education

Management and the Role of Black Managers

John Clark

The Principal of Southall College of Technology, John Clark taught Business Studies at Brixton College from 1975 to 1985 and was Vice-Principal of Southwark College from 1985 to 1989.

I would dearly like to have written an article on multi-cultural education, but I do not know enough about it. I also believe we need many more black staff before the issue can become meaningful. Instead, I will concentrate on management, about which I know something, and racism, about which I know a lot.

In education, joining "management" is considered by many as similar to contracting a social disease and I know that for some readers anything I write from now on will be treated with contempt. On the other hand, joining management can be considered similar to joining a club. Soon after my appointment as Vice-Principal, I attended my first APVP conference (for those not in the club, Association of Principals and Vice-Principals). On my way to the bar I was quizzed by one principal on my knowledge of SSRs, ASHs and numerous other statistics. I was saved from exhibiting too much ignorance by a friendly face who assured me that the principal knew all there was to know about statistics, his only problem was people. In the bar another principal offered to buy me a drink and congratulated me on my appointment. Any illusions I may have had about joining the "club" were shattered when he added, 'Mind you, I would not have appointed you to my college.' Unfortunately, he was not joking.

Because I am a simple soul, I believe that if people in management positions do their jobs properly, they can make a tremendous contribution to anti-racism and multi-cultural education. Having stated that, I suppose I should go through what I consider to be some of the main aspects of management. First, I believe management to be proactive, making things happen, rather than reactive. Management is not administration; different skills are required. I get the impression that many appointment panels have difficulty in understanding the distinction. They appoint administrators and then can't understand why organisations are not managed effectively.

In my view, one of the basic aspects of management is leadership. This may appear to be a rather outmoded concept but it is very important for people, both inside and outside the college, to see the managers take the leading role. In many circumstances this role can be delegated, but it should be understood by all that it has been delegated for a specified project or length of time only. A manager who delegates the leadership role indefinitely ceases to be a manager. In such a circumstance colleagues will very quickly avoid the de jure manager and go direct to the de facto manager. The long-term consequences are that the manager-in-name-only becomes very selective in his or her interest and the vacuum created is filled by someone who takes the leadership role without needing to accept the responsibility. It would be very pleasant to have the glory without the blame, but that does not lead to effective management.

From the leadership/responsibility requirements comes the setting of the style or the ethos of an institution. I am not suggesting that you get a picture of a college by meeting the principal, but the principal and other managers play a vital role. It is not possible for managers to remain aloof from what is happening in their institution.

The aspect of management that I believe most clearly distinguishes managers from administrators is risk. Without taking risks none of us would reach our potential because we would be operating merely within safe limits. To allow for this potential to be reached, managers have to be able to take risks themselves and allow colleagues to do likewise. I cannot see what is wrong with making a few mistakes. The job of the manager is to set the limits within which risks are taken and to be aware of the consequences. In other words, the risks can be calculated.

One area of management that we hear a lot about at the moment is marketing. Recently I upset someone from a higher education establishment by suggesting that marketing was very straightforward and not difficult or sophisticated (I think perhaps he taught marketing). However, I felt I was on strong ground as I had set up and run the market intelligence unit at Sainsbury's for a number of years before coming into teaching. My role was to research markets and recommend products or changes in the product mix. In supermarkets, marketing or market research is not particularly sophisticated, but it is a vital part of management. I would like to consider what would happen if we gave it the same vital role in education.

The first stage in marketing is to understand your customers. If colleges understood their clients, many of whom are black, anti-racism and multi-ethnic education would not be an issue. However, the application of knowledge of the client and his or her needs would, at the moment, require radical changes in the curriculum and many of the staff required to deliver the curriculum would have to be black. We are a long way from this. Some time ago I was involved with the Further Education Unit project "Towards a Non-Racist Curriculum". We found that the black researchers were not accepted in some colleges. Managers who cannot accept highly qualified researchers will of course have great difficulty understanding the needs of young, unqualified, black people.

Management is a function and not a group of people. It is not good enough to classify management as those of head of department status and above. All staff who perform management functions are managers. Course tutors manage in that they undertake all the tasks I have outlined plus many others. In the same way that principals are not able to be selective in their responsibilities, neither are course tutors. On many occasions I have heard the cry that something is 'the management's problem' when the manager concerned is the course tutor. I labour this point because the course teams, led by the tutor, often decide the content of the course. It is in this management role that many staff can have an influence on the anti-racist approaches and the multi-cultural content of courses.

The problem of "them and us" in Britain is, as we all know, woven into the fabric of our society. We just do not value each other or what other people do. In teaching we are even more aware of this because our whole profession is undervalued. However, because some staff treat whatever managers do with contempt, the managers become frightened, not just of making mistakes but of doing anything that may upset the status quo or go against custom and practice.

I find the view that something should not be changed because it has been done in a particular way for years irritating. I also believe it is destructive. Our client groups have changed dramatically over the years and yet we continue to make our traditional offer. It is possible to design our service to meet the needs of our clients in terms of the curriculum, presentation and timing, without worsening teachers' conditions.

Having talked about management and managers generally, I would now like to consider black managers. I assume, in this publication, that there is no need to argue that many more black managers are needed. At the moment major problems arise just because there are not enough of us. We are all expected to be experts in multi-cultural education. I said before that I am not but, because I am black, nobody believes me. The same people who insist that black managers are experts in multi-cultural education are not able to accept our expertise in areas where we do have a great deal of knowledge. White managers do not have to continually explain and justify their backgrounds and experience. The extra scrutiny that we have to undergo is a classic example of racism. Recently a very senior person in the higher education establishment used a number of terms to describe me, including 'very bright young man'. He also worried about my being too laid back. It is not modesty which makes me admit that I am neither very bright nor young! He would not have used such a phrase if I had been white. As to his view that perhaps I am too laid back; well, of course I am laid back – I am a black man. I spent years practising being laid back – it's called survival in a hostile world. The man concerned was not being nasty and he is certainly not a racist; but his attitude is typical of a middle-aged white manager. He simply has not had relevant experience in dealing with black people at his level.

This leads me to talk about the job I went for at an enlightened polytechnic. The polytechnic has a very high proportion of black students but was not able to raise one black person for the selection panel. The job was Assistant Director. I don't believe that the people on the panel had enough experience to interview black people. I am sure that some of them thought I was a 'young man', even if not very bright. You could put my criticism down to sour grapes because I did not get the job, but really it isn't that. I am an old pro' who is quite used to such situations and, to be honest, I was quite sure before I went in that I would not get the job. I am also sure that the poly would not interview women with an all-male panel. What really concerns me is that panels like that will be interviewing young black people who are very well qualified but new to the system and expecting much more. This is one of the aspects of selection that has to be changed to attract the people we need and should want.

Although the polytechnic did not appoint me, they did appoint another black person on secondment. When asked if I would consider a secondment I refused as a matter of principle. It really is not good enough for black people to be on secondments and short-term Section II posts and so on. To me this is not a commitment from an institution to change its management to suit or match its clients' needs more realistically. It simply puts one further burden on black people – toeing the line in case the contract is not renewed.

In general it appears that white people in management have a fear of black people at the same level. There are a number of exceptions and I certainly consider my own college to be in this category. The fear seems to be that we might gain that most precious of commodities – power. This is highlighted by the ongoing drama in the Labour Party over black sections.

I hope that I have highlighted some useful points. Management has a major contribution to make in terms of anti-racism and multi-cultural education. More people are involved in management than like to admit it, and we need to move on from preserving all of the old customs and practices. We must have more black managers; they are out there and we must attract them or we will lose them to other agencies. Lastly, it is vital that the few of us in management do not sell out but keep fighting, no matter how pessimistic we may be at times.

Part III:
Comments

A Black Perspective

Clem Derrick

Clem Derrick is the Manager of one of the ILEA's divisional social work offices. His department oversees the education of children in Hackney and deals with matters such as children's non-attendance.

There is no doubt that black people have played a decisive role in shaping the educational and political perspectives of Britain's capital. The concrete advances we have made within the Authority have been seen by the government as a direct threat to the status quo. Those in power have now taken decisive measures to curtail our political influence within inner city areas by the introduction of the poll tax and the abolition of the GLC and the ILEA. It is clear to me that these ill-conceived measures will rebound on the government.

The government's stance on South Africa and its treatment of black people in Britain are connected. Racism is at the heart of the matter, and the struggle to end racism in the curriculum is politically bound up with the struggle for democracy in Britain. The black community cannot accept reassuring platitudes about how things are; our struggle is to change the existing social order, socially, economically and politically.

Racism and discrimination against black people have been made worse by the government's policies. Racism in Britain is a manifestation of Britain's imperial and colonial legacy. It involves a fundamental denial by white people of the basic human rights of black people. It also manifests itself in a multitude of myths and dogmas which purport to explain racial differences. These range from biblical explanations to zoological classifications. As one explanation loses its novelty, or its power to convince people, another emerges; and what race theorists fail to establish on the basis of measurable physical differences they try to explain in terms of inherent psychological differences. These quasi-scientific approaches to black children have been the basis of much of the ILEA School Psychological Services Practice over the last two decades. Much work has been done by the ILEA's Equal Opportunities Unit and ILEA Members to challenge the foundation of this service's philosophy, working assumptions and practices.

The powerlessness and prejudice which racism generates are reflected in the whole of society, through ideological, social, political and economic arrangements. This is evident in the institutions of state power: Parliament, county and local councils, civil services, the judiciary, educational establishments and the media. All of these institutions overwhelmingly represent a partial interest which does not reflect the popular consensus in society. It is no wonder that black youngsters feel frustrated and alienated from the so-called democratic process.

There is a drastic need for a philosophy of education to redress the imbalances in society. What is education if not a process for the development of intellectual growth and awareness? It could be considered analogous to the growth of a seed into a full-grown plant; it must have light, air and moisture in order to grow. Its future is largely prescribed by its antecedent nature and external conditions. Traditional school methods and subjects have failed to take into account the diversity of talents and need that exists in different human beings. Conformity becomes the criterion by which the pupil is judged in spite of the fact that initiative, originality and independence are precious qualities in the life of a young person. Too many black children are labelled disruptive and maladjusted and are consequently suspended. Teachers should not operate as magistrates set on high, masked by arbitrary authority. They should act as friendly co-partners and guides in a common educational enterprise.

Theories and practices in education have been both varied and numerous. However, any philosophy of education will ultimately be tested by objective evidence. Education is an important determinant of the life and livelihood of individuals, a social distributor of life chances. It is the strongest force on the side of social and redistributive justice. Our schools must be concerned to maximise the potential of individuals.

Racism has systematically denied black people their political and democratic rights. There are many within the ILEA who, whilst acknowledging the existence of racial discrimination, seek to minimise the experience. Over the last few years the most significant challenge to the existing ideological function of schools has come from the black community and black Members of the ILEA. Their active opposition to the racist, classist and sexist nature of the education system has created opportunities for other social groups to look critically at the educational system from their own standpoint. Against this background, and the feeling on the part of many working-class people that comprehensive schools have not delivered the goods, a divisional and borough strategy should be constructed based on an alliance of the white working class, the black community and the progressive and democratic forces in education. Central to this shift in thinking must be a clear strategy for establishing a partnership between the educational authority and the community.

The possibilities for developing a broad, anti-racist, democratic alliance between the different forces in the community are now enormous – if only we can realise that the apparent differences between black and white people are contrived by the outdated social order. There is at present a battle being waged between the black community and the status quo about the nature and role of education. There are those who believe that the white working class and the black community must remain in their present state if they are to meet their needs. They foster racial theories in the curriculum and they actively deprive the community of resources to solve the problems. It is important to note that schools are not simply places where existing divisions are reproduced mechanically. Both teachers and pupils respond in active and dialectical ways to the situations in which they find themselves. Thus, in the past, some progressive teachers have struggled on a national level to challenge the general ethos of schooling through the campaigns for comprehensive education. The present campaign to change schools by the black community must be seen as part of that campaign for a fully comprehensive education.

The ILEA has constantly suffered at the hands of the government and the media, but 1990 will pose extraordinary demands and pressures on those local authorities responsible for education for the first time. I believe that a crisis of confidence is virtually inevitable. To limit potential damage, rational and coherent leadership by the new directors of education during the preliminary period should be a top priority. The various interests and competing forces within education will be attempting to carve up the limited resources. In some ways, day-to-day stability will be maintained through the institutions, where the staff will be relatively "secure" and committed. In order for the local education committees to be effective, united and coherent they should not be fragmented between many administrative departments of the council.

Within the ILEA there has been little direct Member involvement in day-to-day matters as this has generally been channelled through County Hall to the local Divisions. This has given staff, both professional and administrative, a greater autonomy and independence. The ILEA's sole brief has been to run an education service independently of local authority services. Education must now be viewed in a broader context. The ILEA's policy formulation and subsequent implementation has involved an additional hierarchy of officers based at County Hall. By removing this level, the local education authorities' policy formulation should be more responsive to "public demand", and the policies' subsequent implementation should be closer to the intentions of the policymakers.

It is important for us not to lose sight of the horizon or the important initiatives in which we took part at the ILEA. It seems appropriate to say that unless boroughs take on the positive aspects of the ILEA, especially its equal opportunities policies, they will be turning the clock backwards and swimming against the tide.

A Senior Primary School Inspector

Yvonne Conolly

Yvonne Conolly *was the ILEA's first black headteacher, at Ring Cross Infant School in north London, before becoming an Inspector in 1978. She is currently the Senior Primary Schools Inspector for the London Borough of Islington.*

One of the few areas in which black parents and educationalists agree is that the relative underachievement of black children in education is unacceptable. Parents have consistently expressed their desire to have values such as strict discipline and a sense of order, values which many of them experienced in their own schooling in the Caribbean, incorporated into their children's education in Britain. They have also stressed the necessity of appointing teachers who set good examples for their children and who hold high expectations of them as learners.

Most black parents place a high value on education, believing that it is the gateway to further opportunities for their children. They believe that the white people who achieve in this society are almost all products of effective schooling, and that it is the school's function to convince their pupils that with earnest endeavour, they too can achieve. It is hardly surprising that parents are worried when the evidence shows that their children are often barely literate or numerate, nor is it unreasonable that they react with disbelief when teachers tell them that the children's progress is satisfactory.

Parents' dissatisfaction with the standard of their children's education becomes alarming when one considers the plethora of policy initiatives, reports, studies and projects which have been specifically undertaken by the ILEA over the years in order to bring about opportunities for achievement in the black and ethnic minority communities. In 1981 the ILEA examined the levels of achievement of pupils in terms of their race, sex and social class. This led to the 1983 Policy for Equality and multi-ethnic education was redefined to include the perspectives of anti-racism and race equality for all pupils and students. These initiatives acknowledged many of the Authority's concerns, such as the need to value black people's cultural identities and their bilingual competence, and to promote a mutual respect between cultures. It also emphasised the need for addressing the issues of racism and discrimination and their effect on both black and white people. Although the ILEA's initiatives succeeded in increasing its consultation and liaison with black and ethnic minority groups, and in providing support for community endeavours such as supplementary schools, there is no evidence of improved achievement amongst black pupils.

Three further enquiries commissioned by the ILEA, *Improving Primary Schools, Improving Secondary Schools* and *Equal Opportunities for All?*, each confirmed the concerns voiced by black parents over the years – that factors other than ability were contributing to the underachievement of an already disadvantaged group of pupils. The reports pointed to factors such as under-expectation, lack of motivation, insufficient individual attention and the need for more appropriate work to match the range of abilities of individual pupils. I believe that the ILEA's intention to counter black underachievement became blurred and was eventually lost in a general zealousness which focused single-mindedly on the elimination of racism without explicitly linking it to a strategy for improving the children's education. This was because the Authority overlooked the need to spell out the principles which underpin good education and the importance of showing that anti-racist and multi-ethnic approaches are essentially related to the progress children make at school.

The Authority's initiatives did result in a heightened awareness of its anti-racist policy, but there was widespread misunderstanding among teachers about how the policy was supposed to work. In some cases, teachers taking a staunch anti-racist stand gave an interpretation to meeting 'the different needs of black and ethnic minority communities' that was seriously questionable, having little if any relationship to matters such as the kind of behaviour that would be tolerated within a school or the kind of teaching that would motivate children to learn. On the other hand there have been good examples of schools which successfully linked strategies for countering racism and sexism to considerations of good educational practice.

The introduction of the ILEA's equal opportunities policy through a "top-down" model added suspicion to the national confusion surrounding the issue of anti-racism and the ways in which its principles could be used to shape educational practice for the benefit of the pupils. The dissolution of the ILEA and the transfer of education to the boroughs presents a splendid opportunity to reappraise the questions of quality, equality and underachievement. What then are the key areas of thinking in equal opportunities that the boroughs should heed?

Firstly, there is a need for the boroughs to publish a clear, unequivocal policy to show where they stand on equal opportunities for their education service. Boroughs need to show that they recognise that discrimination in terms of race, gender, disabilities and class takes place, and that they have a plan to actively counter it.

Secondly, the link between an equal opportunities perspective and good education practice for all pupils should be explicitly stated. The ways in which the curriculum, bilingualism, training and employment practices will bring about strategies for delivering equal opportunities should be clear and coherently balanced with other developments. This would help all teachers to understand the reasoning behind the policy and enable them to implement it effectively.

Thirdly, there is the need to ensure that teachers understand that increasing children's achievement is the main goal of the work they do. They need to be persuaded that it is hard work, not innate ability, that produces educational achievement. Schools which are unselectively effective will be favoured by all parents alike.

Fourthly, there is a need for a shift in the moral tone used by many well-intentioned teachers, particularly in anti-racist and multi-ethnic education. The temptation to personalise anti-racist and equal opportunities issues to the point of suggesting that nothing can be achieved until racism is eliminated must be discouraged. Equal opportunities policies are as much about providing equality for groups of people who are disadvantaged by various kinds of discrimination as they are about meeting the needs of individuals within those groups.

Fifthly, every borough will need to create structures which enable them to listen to the parents and involve them in the work of the borough and the school.

Black children need to have the opportunity to achieve, even in the face of racism. As one parent was heard to remark, 'Fighting racism must also be about ensuring that our children can think, ask questions and be literate and numerate, so that they can fight that racism with intelligence and style – even if they can't win the battle.'

Appendix

Appendix I

The structure of the ILEA

POLICY MAKING

The policies to be pursued by the Authority are, as for other local authorities, decided by the elected members. The ILEA is composed of 58 members with two representatives for each of the 29 parliamentary constituencies in inner London. The most recent composition has been Labour 45, Conservative 11, Social and Liberal Democrats 1, with one vacancy.

Leading Members of the ILEA

Chair	Tony Powell
Vice-Chair	Les Francis
Leader	Neil Fletcher
Deputy Leader	Anstey Rice
Chief Whip	Lesley Hammond
Deputy Chief Whips	Peter Willsman
	Jim Mthethwa
Further & Higher Education	Paul Flather
Schools	Martin Rogers
Staff	Deirdre Wood
Staff Appeals	Charlie Rossi
Strategic Policy	Neil Fletcher
Opposition Leader	Eric Ollerenshaw
Deputy Leader of the Opposition	Margaret Riddell
Opposition Chief Whip	Herbert Sandford

Chairs of Sub-Committees

Development	John O'Malley
Equal Opportunities	Lorna Boreland-Kelly
Finance	June Ward

Administrative Structure of the ILEA

Chief Executive: Herman Ouseley
Education Officer: David Mallen

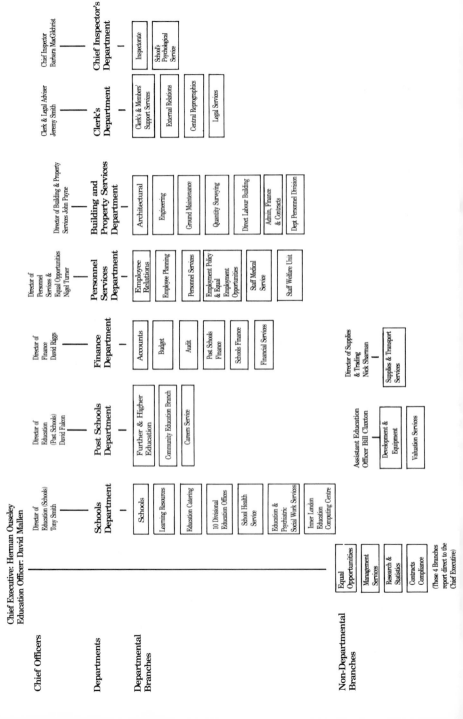

Chief Officers

| Director of Education (Schools) Tony Smith | Director of Education (Post Schools) David Faxon | Director of Finance David Riggs | Director of Personnel Services & Equal Opportunities Nigel Turner | Director of Building & Property Services John Payne | Clerk & Legal Adviser Jeremy Smith | Chief Inspector Barbara MacGilchrist |

Departments

| Schools Department | Post Schools Department | Finance Department | Personnel Services Department | Building and Property Services Department | Clerk's Department | Chief Inspector's Department |

Departmental Branches

Schools	Further & Higher Education	Accounts	Employee Relations	Architectural	Clerk's & Members' Support Services	Inspectorate
Learning Resources	Community Education Branch	Budget	Employee Planning	Engineering	External Relations	School's Psychological Service
Education Catering	Careers Service	Audit	Personnel Services	Ground Maintenance	Central Reprographics	
10 Divisional Education Offices		Post Schools Finance	Employment Policy & Equal Employment Opportunities	Quantity Surveying	Legal Services	
School Health Service		Schools Finance	Staff Medical Service	Direct Labour Building		
Education & Psychiatric Social Work Services		Financial Services	Staff Welfare Unit	Admin, Finance & Contracts		
Inner London Education Computing Centre				Dept Personnel Division		

Director of Supplies & Trading Nick Sharman

Supplies & Transport Services

Assistant Education Officer Bill Claxton

Development & Equipment

Valuation Services

Non-Departmental Branches

Equal Opportunities

Management Services

Research & Statistics

Contracts Compliance

(These 4 Branches report direct to the Chief Executive)

Appendix II

Equal Opportunities Publications Produced by ILEA's Equal Opportunities Inspectorate/Advisory Team

Equal Opportunities and Achievement in the Primary School,
Pana McGee, 1986.
Equal Opportunities in the Early Years of School: Conference Report,
Avery Hill, 20-22 June
1986, Linda Magill, 1986.
Equal Opportunities in the First Year Pastoral Curriculum, Mary Parker,
1986.
First Reflections: Equal Opportunities in Early Years, Linda Magill, 1986.
Further Concerns: Some Approaches To Equal Opportunities in Further
Education, 1987.
Implementing Equal Opportunities for Girls and Boys Through
'Improving Secondary
Schools': Paper, Carol Adams, 1985.
Implementing the ILEA's Anti-Sexist Policy: A Guide for Colleges of
Further Education,
1986.
Implementing the ILEA's Anti-Sexist Policy: A Guide for Schools, 1986.
Implementing the ILEA's Anti-Sexist Policy: A Guide for Youth Clubs,
Youth Projects, Youth
Centres, Play Centres and Junior Clubs in the Youth Service, 1986.
Implementing the ILEA's Anti-Sexist Policy: Guidelines for Adult
Education Institutes and
Community Education Centres, 1986.
Investigating Gender in Primary Schools: Activity-Based INSET
Materials for Primary
Teachers, compiled by Carol Adams and Valerie Walkerdine, 1986.
Investigating Gender in Secondary Schools: A Series of In-Service
Workshops for ILEA
Teachers, compiled by Carol Adams and Madeleine Arnot, 1986.
Primary Matters: Some Approaches to Equal Opportunities in Primary
Schools, 1986.

Providing In-Service Training in Equal Opportunities: Conference Report, Isledon Teachers' Centre, January 1984, 1984.
Reluctant Masters: Essays By 15 Women in the Open University M.A. in Education Gender and Education Module, 1988, 1989.
Secondary Issues? Some Approaches to Equal Opportunities in Secondary Schools, 1986.
Self-Defence for Girls and Young Women and Assertiveness Training in Schools, Maria Jastrzebska and Anne Hordyk, 1987, revised edition, forthcoming 1990.
Single Sex Groupings in Mixed Schools: A Discussion Document and Case Studies, Carol Adams and Sybil Naidu, 1987.
Stop, Look and Listen: An Account of Girls' and Boys' Achievement in Reading and Mathematics in the Primary School, Pip Osmont and Jenny Davis, 1987.
Supporting Adults Learning: Information from Four Further Education Colleges, compiled by Ceri Williams, forthcoming 1990.
Tackling Inequalities: Work With Men, Stan Grant, forthcoming 1990.
The 'Thomas Report' and Sex Equality: Paper, Carol Adams, 1985.
Visiting Teachers for Equal Opportunities at the Institute of Education, 1986-7; Report, 1987.
Women Return to Learning: A Guide to Education and Training in Inner London, Ceri Williams, 1990.
Women's Self-Defence: Paper, Judith Lowe, 1990.
Working the System: Equal Opportunities Work in Colleges, compiled by Sue Karahalli, forthcoming 1990.